Learning to Learn

A GUIDE TO BECOMING INFORMATION LITERATE

Ann Marlow Riedling

Introduction by **Michael Eisenberg**

Neal-Schuman Publishers, Inc.

New York   London

> **Don't miss this book's**
> **companion Web site**
> **www.neal-schuman.com/riedling**

Published by Neal-Schuman Publishers, Inc.
100 Varick Street
New York, NY 10013

The paper used in this publication meets the minimum requirements of American National Standard for Information Sciences—Permanence of Paper for Printed Library Materials, ANSI Z39.48–1992. ∞

ISBN 1-55570-452-2

Library of Congress Cataloging-in-Publication Data available. Record number 2002026532

Contents

List of Figures

Foreword

Anyone who knows me knows that I am passionate in my work about two things: information literacy and libraries. I firmly believe that information literacy is essential to the success of everyone in our world, and that libraries are key institutions for ensuring that people become information literate. To me, information literacy is the 4th R; it's not enough anymore to be able to read, write, and do math. People need to be able to analyze their information needs and find, evaluate, and use the requisite information. That's what the Big6 approach to information and technology skills is all about, and we've got a long way to go to make information literacy learning a reality.

Learning to Learn is another step forward in the effort to make learning information skills an attainable goal. I am pleased to write this foreword to Ann Marlow Riedling's new book.

Learning to Learn succinctly lays out the steps and approaches to information literacy, from beginning to end. She writes, "information literacy is the ability to access, evaluate, organize, and use information." To this end, *Learning to Learn* takes the reader from what it means to be information literate, through research planning, finding information, using information resources (for example, libraries and the Internet), evaluation, copyright and plagiarism, citation styles, to general writing skills.

At its center, being information literate means "understanding the how, what, why, when, and where about the information with which you are presented." As Ann Riedling recognizes, this is the evolving nature of our understanding about the marriage of information and learning. A true learner must be an information literate person, and will continually add to their skills and abilities to conduct research—to frame questions as well as find and use information to resolve those questions.

Learning to Learn will be a valuable tool in the broad sense, but also in its ability to lead individual learners down the ever-widening path to information literacy. We're not talking here about the "fad of the month" that sometimes seems to pervade education and library work. *Learning to Learn* is enduring.

Michael B. Eisenberg

Michael B. Eisenberg (PhD, Syracuse University, MLS, State University of New York at Albany) is the Dean of the Information School at the University of Washington and a prolific author on the subject of information literacy. He is nationally known for his innovative approach to problem-solving and critical thinking/information and technology skills development: the Big6 Skills. For many years, Dr. Eisenberg was Director of the Information Institute of Syracuse, which includes the ERIC Clearinghouse on Information & Technology and the award-winning AskERIC service.

Preface

Whether you are researching car repair costs or looking for stock tips, you face an unprecedented amount of information from an amazing variety of information-seeking tools. Will you master information literacy skills and learn to have information serve your needs or will you struggle with a "fire hose blast" of information that you cannot sift through? *Learning to Learn* is designed as a hands-on, step-by-step companion workbook to be used with information literacy classes to help learners master essential skills.

Learning to Learn shows you the way to cut through all the useless information and get right to what matters. Through explanations, exercises, and explorations of some of the greatest sites on the Web, this book covers the "entire process" of research. The chapters are arranged in a sequential order. However, if you need help with a particular aspect of research, the relevant chapter can be read outside the context of the preceding chapters.

I have tried to present a wide assortment of some of the best, interactive research-oriented information literacy sites currently available on the Web. To make your search for these sites quick and easy, and to keep the links up to date, I have hyperlinked them all in one spot on the *Learning to Learn* section of Neal-Schuman's Web site: (www.neal-schuman.com/riedling).

The site features all the figures in this book and an easy-to-download collection of useful links and exercises providing additional training regarding various areas of information literacy, research, and education.

Here's a chapter-by-chapter breakdown of *Learning to Learn*:

Chapter 1: What Does It Mean To Be Information Literate? discusses the critical nature of new research skills. Several information/problem-solving models are provided to illustrate the research/learning process.

Chapter 2: I Am Ready To Research. Where Do I Start? covers subject selection, narrowing a subject to a topic, and basic resources and tools necessary to locate an appropriate topic. After studying this chapter you won't feel overwhelmed or start your project discouraged.

Chapter 3: How Do I Find the Information I Need? examines the search for information. This includes proper organization as well as constructive research strategies and techniques. With this knowledge, learning can be much more manageable and lead to great discoveries.

Chapter 4: How Can the Library Help Me? provides useful information about library policies and services, electronic information (including indexes and databases), and virtual libraries. It is important to understand that libraries are constantly adding new technologies and can efficiently provide enormous amounts of valuable information.

Chapter 5: There Is So Much Information on the Internet. Where Do I Begin? explores helpful and resourceful search techniques, search engines, subject directories, and the Invisible (or Deep) Web—and how to use them successfully. "Surfing the Net" without knowledge of where to go is a significant problem for researchers today.

Chapter 6: How Do I Know If What I Read Is the Truth? covers the evaluation of information. With the emergence of new and immeasurable amounts of information (that can be provided by literally anyone), savvy evaluation of information is imperative.

Chapter 7: What Are Copyright and Plagiarism All About? discusses the extremely important and often overlooked issues of copyright and plagiarism of print, nonprint, and Internet resources. You must become aware that infringements of copyright—and plagiarism—are not only dishonest but illegal.

Chapter 8: How Do I Give Credit to the Creator of the Information I Read? explains three basic citation styles, *Chicago Manual of Style, MLA Handbook for Writers of Research Papers,* and *Publication Manual of the American Psychological Association.* Giving proper credit to the creators of information is an extremely important facet of research and learning.

Chapter 9: Now That I've Finished the Research, How Do I Write the Paper? provides methods, guidelines, and examples to assist you with organizing research information. This chapter also discusses analyzing, proofreading, and editing form and format as they apply to a well-written, high-quality research paper.

I hope *Learning to Learn* will become a much-consulted map as you learn your information literacy skills. Once you gain knowledge of how to *learn to learn* by improving your ability to perform specific tasks, an awesome new world will open up and beckon you to explore and grow.

A Note to Instructors

Learning to Learn can function as a practical manual or guidebook for students of any age interested in acquiring or expanding information literacy (IL) proficiencies. I designed it as a companion workbook suitable for a wide range of basic IL classes; from middle and high school through undergraduate and graduate university classes. This book will provide students with the basics of information literacy, information access, and research to strive and thrive in today's increasingly complicated world of information gathering.

Many young people have had only limited contact with the benefits of the computer revolution. Educators learn daily that even students fortunate enough to have access to computers often do not have the commiserate skills to use them successfully. How many students from either group understand how to creatively combine the use of digital and print research? A great number of students in our society are utterly unprepared with regard to effective and efficient learning. Those with more abilities benefit from constant skill reinforcement. I wrote *Learning to Learn* to be a useful and valuable instructional guide for all people wishing to expand their knowledge about research and learning in the twenty-first century through interesting and engaging discussions, helpful exercises, and explorations of interactive Web sites.

This guide differs from other books in that it communicates the entire process of the research experience, while allowing students to practice via authentic and relevant exercises. The chapters start with the essential background of information literacy, move systematically through the various stages of finding a research topic and learning how to explore it effectively, and then turn to the process of making this information into a paper that will support the unique ideas and talents of the individual student. Along the way, we stop and explore key issues of research:

- How do libraries and librarians help? How do you determine if your source is valid?

- What do you need to know about plagiarism and copyright?
- How do you give credit properly?

Learning to Learn tries to present the entire range of research in a workable way. Other textbooks may focus on specific topics (for instance, problem-solving models) or a particular audience (for example, high school students). This is a book for anyone interested in conducting research, using technologies of today's world, and wanting to learn to learn.

As an instructor, feel free to expand or modify any of the exercises presented here or simply use them as a springboard for ideas intrinsic to your own lesson plans. Most exercises can be developed with differing Web sites and a variety of teaching methods to create further knowledge and interest. Remember that you are only limited by your imagination!

Be sure to visit the *Learning to Learn* companion Web site. Here you will find all the Web sites examined in this guide hyperlinked (and updated) all in one handy spot.

I believe your students will enjoy this textbook. I trust it will make the exciting challenge of *learning to learn* more enjoyable for you, too.

Acknowledgments

There are five special people I want to thank for this book:

Thank you, Charles Harmon, Director of Publishing, Neal-Schuman Publishers, Inc., for believing in me and the importance of this book.

Thank you, Michael Kelley, Development and Production Editor, Neal-Schuman Publishers, Inc., for absolutely brilliant and insightful editing, as well as support and encouragement that cannot be matched.

Thank you, Dr. Michael Eisenberg, for writing the foreword for this book. The words you write are dear to my heart.

Thank you, Russ, my husband, who provides me with constant assistance, total and unending support and encouragement for all of my endeavors, and the patience of Job. He inspires me to be what I am.

Thank you, Marlow, my daughter, who understands my long hours of work and has constant faith in what I do. She is sunshine every day.

Without these people, this book would not have been possible… and thank God it is, because I believe in it with all my heart. May all who read it understand how to learn and to move forward in the twenty first century.

Chapter 1

What Does It Mean To Be Information Literate?

The quantity and complexity of information we deal with is growing exponentially. The capacity of a human brain holds no more information than it did 500 years ago; yet, the amount of information we have access to has increased in size by thousands, millions...maybe even billions. At one point, people wrote on stone tablets; later the printing press was invented; much later the computer was invented. The expansive media provide us with access to more information than we can ever conceive of—much less view in a lifetime. Our capacity to learn has not grown, but the amount of information we are exposed to has developed beyond imagination. As a result, no education is adequate today unless it helps to increase your ability to deal with the vastness of information.

The ability to access, evaluate, organize, and use information is called *information literacy.* Today information comes in a wide variety of formats (books, videotapes, CD-ROMs, etc.) and is accessible by numerous means. In order to conduct proper and effective research, you must acquire information literacy skills. It was not very long ago that one's research needs could be satisfied with the library catalog and a few reference books and periodicals (if you do not recall this, ask someone over 40 years of age!). You now have online access to a large number of library catalogs, many online periodical databases and indexes, full-text of numerous journals, a wide variety of nonprint resources, and a multitude of Web sites. Because of this, you must now learn new skills and procedures to conduct research—and, *learn to learn,* using these new formats, processes, strategies, and techniques. This chapter will explain two specific research models and refer you to others that can help you make great strides in becoming information literate.

INFORMATION LITERACY

First, it is important to understand that information literacy forms the basis for lifelong learning. Information literacy is common to all disciplines, learning environments, and levels of education. Information literacy enables you to master content, become more self-directed, and assume greater control over your own learning. The abilities to access, comprehend, and use information have become the skills you must develop to function in today's world.

A number of people and organizations have developed definitions of information literacy. According to the American Library Association (1989), information literacy is the ability to access, evaluate, organize, and use information from a variety of sources. Being information literate requires that you:

- know how to clearly define a subject or area of investigation.
- select the appropriate terminology to express the concept or subject under investigation.
- formulate a search strategy that takes into consideration different sources of information and the various ways of organizing information.
- analyze your data for value, relevancy, quality, and suitability, and can subsequently turn information into knowledge.

This involves a deeper understanding of how and where to locate information, the ability to judge whether the information is meaningful, and ultimately, how best to use that information to address the problem or issue at hand. With the rapid increase in the amount of information and the increasing availability of information technology, information literacy has quickly become one of the most vital sets of skills for the twenty-first century. The American Association of School Librarians equates information literacy with information power. (See Figure 1.1) What does that mean? It means that you can proficiently use an online library catalog; you understand how to use the Internet effectively to search for information; you can use a computer; you understand that not everything is "free for the taking" (there are copyright laws); you can "think outside of the box," that is, you can think critically and creatively; and you can competently express your thoughts orally and in writing.

Information is available from a variety of resources, including online library databases, electronic magazines, the Internet, books, magazines, journals, etc. As an information literate person, you must know why, how, and when to use each of these resources effectively and efficiently.

INFORMATION POWER

The Nine Information Literacy Standards
for Student Leaning

Excerpted from Chapter 2, "Information Literacy Standards for Student Learning," of *Information Power: Building Partnerships for Learning.*

Information Literacy

Standard 1: The student who is information literate accesses information efficiently and effectively.

Standard 2: The student who is information literate evaluates information critically and competently.

Standard 3: The student who is information literate uses information accurately and creatively.

Independent Learning

Standard 4: The student who is an idependent learner is information literate and pursues information related to personal interests.

Standard 5: The student who is an independent learner is information literate and appreciates literature and other creative expressions of information.

Standard 6: The student who is an idependent learner is information literate and strives for excellence in information seeking and knowledge generation.

Social Responsibility

Standard 7: The student who contributes positively to the learning community and to society is information literate and recognizes the importance of information to a democratic society.

Standard 8: The student who contributes positively to the learning community and to society is information literate and practices ethical behavior in regard to information and information technology

Standard 9: The student who contributes positively to the learning community and to society information literate and participates effectively in groups to pursue and generate information.

Figure 1.1 Nine Standards of Information Literacy © 2002 by the American Library Association and the Association for Educational Communications and Technology, *Information Power: Building Partnerships for Learning.* Reprinted by permission.

Let's look at information literacy from a more practical standpoint. As an information literate person, what exactly do you need to be able to do? The following list includes both information literacy skills and an example of each one in use.

- Determine the extent of information needed.
  For example, you might choose Canadian immigration policies as your research topic.
- Access the needed information effectively and efficiently.
  You know to use proper search words, e.g., "Immigration, laws, Canada" when searching for information—or locating an online article or book about the topic.
- Evaluate information and its sources critically.
  You realize that not all information on the Internet is fact—and are able to distinguish fact from fiction.
- Incorporate selected information into one's knowledge base.
  You comprehend this information—truly understand what you are saying.
- Use information effectively to accomplish a specific task.
  You write about immigration laws in Canada based on the resources and information you have located—using a variety of sources.
- Understand the legal and socioeconomic issues surrounding the use of information—access and use information ethically and legally.
  You understand that what you say can have legal implications— you understand copyright, plagiarism, and the effects of the "printed word."

Information literacy is a means to help you learn to deal with today's information explosion. Good decisions depend on good information. Decision-makers of all types must develop perceptive information skills if they are to prosper in today's technological, global society. Being information smart means knowing when you need help and where to find it. A person who is truly information literate will know that real information power is having the right information when you need it. As Peter Drucker (1969), the noted management expert, stated many years ago, the most important thing you will have to learn is how to learn. The most important thing, in other words, is not subject specific skills, but a universal skill—that of using knowledge and its systematic acquisition as the foundation for performance, skill, and achievement.

PROBLEM-SOLVING MODELS

Knowledge seeking is a process that is applicable for any type of information. Self-directed learning skills are critical in your development as a lifelong, independent person. Research models (such as the two mentioned in this section) present research processes and problem-solving skills—necessities for lifelong learning. Remember that the model you adopt is likely to shift as you mature in your own learning styles and abilities. There are two prominent models that describe the problem-solving/research process: *The Big6* by Eisenberg and Berkowitz and the *Research Model Process* by Stripling and Pitts.

The Big6 Skills Model Approach

The *Big6* Model makes it easier to see the connection between the research process and using Internet information sources effectively. The approach focuses on the process of solving information problems. It is a systematic approach to organizing information from a variety of sources. The Big6 is a well-known model and is being taught widely as a guide for research. The Big6 skills approach model is as follows (this is the basic model):

1. Task Definition
   a. Define the problem.
   b. Define the information requirements of the problem.
2. Information Seeking Strategies
   a. Determine the range of possible resources.
   b. Evaluate the different possible resources to determine priorities.
3. Location and Access.
   a. Locate sources.
   b. Find information within resources.
4. Use of information
   a. Engage.
   b. Extract information from a source.
5. Synthesis
   a. Organize information from multiple sources.
   b. Present information.
6. Evaluation
   a. Judge the product.
   b. Judge the information problem-solving process.

The Big6

For additional information, explore the following Web sites:

Information Literacy for the Information Age

www.big6.com

This site is the basis site for the Big6 model.

Nuts and Bolts of the Big6: In Search of Information Literacy

www.kn.pacbell.com/wired/big6

This site includes resources, activities, and games related to the Big6.

What is the Big6?

www.clovisusd.k12.ca.us/alta/big6

This site is a workshop that introduces the Big6 processes.

Think of this practically. You need a car. You only have "x" amount of money to purchase a car. What do you do? The following are probable steps:

- You have already defined the problem—the need for a car.
- You gather information about the problem (cars under "x" amount of money available for purchase).
- You determine possible resources (advertisements, people, newspapers, etc.).
- You locate possible materials about available cars (purchase a newspaper, call a mechanic, visit a friend).
- You use the information about the location of possible cars that you can purchase by visiting the locations (used car lots, homes).
- You look at what you have seen (a 1988 Nissan for "x" amount; a 1999 Ford for "x" amount; and so on).
- You make a decision according to the information you have and buy the car—*based* on the information you have gathered.
- Later you may perhaps evaluate it. Does the car run properly? Have you seen the same type of car for less money? Do you know what to "do better" the next time you look for a car?

The Research Process Model

The Stripling & Pitts Research Process Model was originally developed in 1988. It gained wide acceptance because it provided a guide through each stage of creating a research paper. However, each stage requires reflection on what had just been completed (this is the "basic" research process model):

1. Choose a broad topic.
2. Get an overview of the topic.
3. Narrow the topic.
4. Develop a thesis or statement of purpose.
5. Formulate questions to guide research.
6. Plan for research and production.
7. Find, analyze, and evaluate sources.
8. Evaluate evidence. Take notes. Compile bibliography.
9. Establish connections. Organize information into an outline.
10. Create and present final product.

Research process/problem-solving models are extremely useful and practical tools when conducting research—of any type, by any age group. Proper and successful research goes hand-in-hand with becoming information literate in today's world.

Exercise: Research Problem-Solving Models

Now it is your turn to consider what *you do* when attempting to find information. List your steps in seeking information.

Step 1: _____

Step 2: _____

Step 3: _____
(Add steps as needed.)

Now, try this. Interview a friend, parent, professor, or sibling. Ask that person to explain his or her information-seeking behavior. Note some differences and similarities. List two of each:

Difference: _____

Difference: _____

(continued on next page)

Exercise: Research Problem-Solving Models (*continued*)

Similarity: _____

Similarity: _____

What useful tips did you discover by learning about another person's information seeking behavior? List at least two:

Tip: _____

Tip: _____

Everyone has specific information-seeking behaviors. Your information-seeking behavior is *your* method, strategy, technique for locating and organizing information—all types of information. Let's look at an example. Some people are very organized and precise in how they locate and organize information. John wants to buy a new monitor for his computer. He gets out a piece of paper and lists the steps he will take to locate information about computer monitors.

Step 1: Go to the library and look through some computer magazines.
Step 2: Ask the librarian if she/he knows of any more print sources that explain the different types of computer monitors.
Step 3: Search "AskJeeves" and "Yahoo!" to locate information.
Step 4: Call some friends to discover what they know about monitors.

I bet you are getting the picture, right? While John may be extremely organized in his information seeking behavior, Julie may have a less organized, but equally effective information-seeking behavior.

Did you think everyone looked for information in the same way before completing this exercise?

CONCLUSION

No other change in our nation has offered greater challenges than the emergence of the Information Age. In an information society, you should have the right to information that can enhance your life, but to reap the benefits of our global, technological society, you must be information literate. Our evolving world includes an incredible growth of knowledge, an explosion of technology, and a speedy reconfiguration of the boundaries that separate academic fields and social conventions. This complex society continues to expand at a rate beyond the capacity of individuals to comprehend. Collectively, and with the use of technologies that have potentiated the momentum of change, humanity generates tremendous amounts of information. Access to information is vital to ease the burden of change and to help society navigate its course toward the future. The abilities to access, comprehend, evaluate, and use information are the skills you must develop in order to function in our world today. To become information literate is to *learn to learn!*

REFERENCES AND FURTHER READING

Allen, Christine. 1999. *Skills for Life: Information Literacy for Grades K–6* (2nd ed.). Worthington, OH: Linworth.

Allen, Christine, and Mary Alice Anderson. 1999. *Skills for Life: Information Literacy for Grades 7–12* (2nd ed.). Worthington, OH: Linworth.

American Association of School Librarians and Association for Educational Communications and Technology. 1998. *Information Power: Guidelines for School Library Media Programs*. Chicago: American Library Association.

American Association of School Librarians and the Association for Educational Communications and Technology. 1996. *Information Standards for Student Learning*. Washington, DC: Authors.

American Library Association. 1989. *ALA Presidential Committee on Information Literacy: Final Report*. Chicago: American Library Association.

Andronik, Catherine. 2000. *Information Literacy Skills, Grades 7–12* (3rd ed.). Worthington, OH: Linworth.

Barren, Daniel D. 2001. "Thanks for the Connections...Now Are We Information Literate?" *School Library Media Activities Monthly*, 18: 49.

Bleakley, Anne, and Jackie L. Carrigan. 1994. *Resource-Based Learning Activities: Information Literacy for High School Students*. Chicago: American Library Association.

Brown, Barbara J. 1995. *The Good Detective's Guide to Library Research*. New York: Neal-Schuman.

Drucker, Peter. 1969. *The Age of Discontinuity: Guidelines to Our Changing Society*. New York: Harper and Row.

Eisenberg, Michael B., and Robert E. Berkowitz. 2000. *The Big6 Collection: The Best of the Big6 Newsletter.* Worthington, OH: Linworth.

Ercegovac, Zorona. 2001. *Information Literacy, Search Strategies, Tools and Resources for High School Students*. Worthington, OH: Linworth.

Grassian, Esther, and Joan Kaplowitz. 2001. *Information Literacy Instruction: Theory and Practice.* New York: Neal-Schuman.

Ishizuka, Kathy, Walter Minkel, and Walter St. Lifer. 2001. "5 Biggest Challenges for 2002." *School Library Journal*, 48: 50.

Joyce, Marilyn Z., and Julie I. Tallman. 1997. *Making the Writing and Research Connection with the I-Search Process.* New York: Neal-Schuman.

Loertscher, David V., and Blanche Woolls. 1999. *Information Literacy: A Review of the Research.* San Jose, CA: Hi Willow.

Logan, Debra Kay. 1999. *Information Skills Toolkit: Collaborative Integrated Instruction for the Middle Grades.* Worthington, OH: Linworth.

Milam, Peggy. 2001. *Information Quest: A New Twist on Information Literacy.* Worthington, OH: Linworth.

Quaratiello, Arlene Rodda. 2000. *The College Student's Research Companion, Second Edition.* New York: Neal-Schuman.

Stripling, Barbara K., and Judy M. Pitts. 1988. *Brainstorms and Blueprints: Teaching Library Research as a Thinking Process.* Englewood, CO: Libraries Unlimited.

Thomas, Nancy Pickering. 1999. *Information Literacy and Information Skills Instruction.* Greenwood Village, CO: Libraries Unlimited.

Chapter 2

I Am Ready To Research.
Where Do I Start?

It is likely that you will conduct research many times in your academic and personal life. Courses will require research papers and projects; as an adult you will need to conduct research about specific colleges, banks, jobs, cars, careers, and other topics. The skills you already have, combined with the skills you will learn in this book and those you will continue to develop, will make the process of research much easier. In this chapter, you will "prewrite" your research paper by:

- differentiating between a subject and a topic;
- generating ideas for a research topic and deciding on a topic;
- developing a thesis statement;
- becoming aware of where and how to locate resources for your topic;
- learning to focus;
- collecting useful, accurate information; and
- utilizing various tools and techniques for successful writing.

Writing a research paper or collecting the information that you need to make an important personal financial decision can be quite intimidating. It helps to break it down into steps. This chapter will guide you through these steps and get you started.

SUBJECTS AND TOPICS

A *subject* is an expansive area of interest. Examples of subjects are education, sports, animals, medicine, etc. These subjects are much too large to research effectively. Therefore, you must narrow the large area (subject) to a smaller area (topic). Selecting a topic is an integral phase of the research process and it requires careful consideration and time. A *topic* can be thought of as a particular question, issue, problem, or concern within a given subject. For example, you might narrow down the subject of education to the topic of home schooling. Another example is the broad subject of violence, which can be narrowed to smaller subjects such as gun control, gangs, or school violence. In order to conduct successful research, you should find a topic that is not too large (you might be overwhelmed with information and not know where to begin) nor too small (you could have difficulty finding enough information on the topic). Choosing topics will become easier with practice.

DISCOVERING IDEAS AND DECIDING ON A TOPIC

Information is all around us. Finding information is not the problem; selecting the best and most relevant information from all that is available is the problem. The first step is to think about a topic that you find interesting or something you would like to learn more about. Your selected topic should also provide you with an opportunity to explore, do original thinking, and make judgments. It is wise to avoid topics for which only limited information is available, those that are extremely controversial, and topics that are overworked (i.e., topics many people have already written about). When defining your topic, the following task may assist you:

- Find a definition of your topic in a dictionary, encyclopedia, or the Internet (e.g., home AND schooling). Write it down.
- Is the definition different from your understanding of the topic? Write down what is new to you.
- What is not clear to you in the definition?
- List any terms or ideas that you do not plainly understand in the definition.

It may also be helpful to visit a library and answer the following questions before deciding on your topic:

- How many titles are listed about the topic in the catalog?
- Is the topic broken down into subheadings in the catalog? It may be beneficial to list any subheadings that you can find.
- How many articles can you locate on the topic? Try a number of

online databases to see what you can locate. (See Chapter 4 for further information concerning online databases.)
- How much information can you find on the Internet? Try a variety of search words (synonyms) and several different search engines. (See Chapter 5 for further information about search engines.)

Where you begin is critical to determining where you will end up and how strong your research will be. Everyone approaches decision making in different ways. You bring your own experiences to the task when selecting topics. It may also be helpful for you to realize that a certain amount of confusion and indecision is to be expected. Possible questions to assist you in selecting a topic are:

- Will the topic hold your interest for several weeks or months?
- Is the topic something about which you already know but can build upon or extend?
- Does the topic fit the requirements of the assignment?
- Is sufficient information available on the topic?
- Do you have adequate time and resources to investigate the topic?

Your mission is to think of possible topics, consider the probable outcome of each, weigh the prospects, and choose one to research.

After deciding on your topic, it is important not to rush or unduly pressure yourself to "dig right in." It takes time for thoughts to develop to the point where you can make an intelligent decision on the research topic. Slow down and consider the topic; think clearly. Again, there are basic steps with regard to locating ideas or topics:

- *Read.* Real writers read a lot—broadly about a variety of areas. This does not merely mean textbooks…or books. Reading of scholarly newspapers, magazines, scholarly journals, and so forth, are excellent sources to broaden your thoughts and ideas.
- *Look for problems, not answers.* When reading, seek out questions and unresolved issues. Take a fresh look at an old issue. Write by using interesting questions and ideas.
- *Record your ideas.* If you don't keep track of what you are thinking, you will most likely forget it. The format for recording your thoughts is not important as long as it works for you.
- *Ask people.* Asking questions is not an indication of ignorance; it shows interest, concern, and the desire to learn. You can learn much from the experience, wisdom, and ideas of others.

Selecting a Topic

For additional ideas, visit the following Web sites:

A Guide to Library Research: Pick a Topic

www.libraries.rutgers.edu/rul/libs/robeson_lib/

This Web site offers additional ideas for topic selection.

Information Studies: Topic Selection

www.accd.edu/pac/lrc/colby/restopic.htm

This site also discusses a variety of methods of generating ideas for topic selection.

Subject Pathfinders

www.valencia.cc.edu/lrcwest/pathfindersub.html

This site is helpful in locating background information on a topic as well as providing an in-depth analysis of the topic.

Exercise: Determining a Topic

Let's practice narrowing a subject into a topic. For example, a subject could be "adolescents"; three topics might be:

1. Adolescents and the use of the drug Ecstasy
2. Adolescents living with an alcoholic parent
3. Homeless adolescents

For the following three subjects, determine three topics each:

Sports

Topic 1: _____

Topic 2: _____

Topic 3: _____

(continued on next page)

Exercise: Determining a Topic *(continued)*

Religion

Topic 1: _____

Topic 2: _____

Topic 3: _____

The Environment

Topic 1: _____

Topic 2: _____

Topic 3: _____

What steps did you take to locate your topics? Did the exercise become easier the more you practiced? Can you think of ways to discover topics more efficiently?

GETTING STARTED

Locating Information About Your Topic

You have selected your topic and you are ready to learn more about it. Information on your topic is available from books, print and online periodicals, print and online newspapers, the Internet, listservs, e-mails, and by talking to others. Your choice of sources will depend on your research. For instance, if you are looking for tomorrow's weather, you might consult a local newspaper; if you are looking for a good movie to see, you could consult a friend; if you are looking for information on a country in the Middle East, you may perhaps consult a book, print or online journal, newspaper, or the Internet.

Learning to Focus

Once you have selected your topic, the next process is to explore information on the general topic in search of a focus for your research. A focus may be one aspect of the general topic that you choose to concentrate on, or it may be a central theme within the topic. Forming a focus for research marks a turning point in the research process. Before you form a focus, you gather general information on your topic. After you decide on a focus, you gather specific information about your area of focus. The way to do this is to explore several possible choices and decide on one that appears to promise the most success. The focus of the topic should be an aspect that you find particularly interesting and thought provoking. It should motivate you and encourage you to gather and form ideas and opinions about the topic.

There may be more than one direction in which you can develop your topic—each of these possibilities needs to be explored. Library resources to identify and focus your topic are vital to your research success. Remember, however, that different sources of information may present opposing or conflicting views that seem unconnected and inconsistent. You must identify a unifying thread or theme for your research. Exploring many possible choices forms a focus and deciding on the particular/specific focus will determine the direction your research will take. All of this is critical before proceeding with your information collection. Although a definite focus should be formed at this point in the research process, the focus need not remain static; it may continue to take shape as long as the research continues. Before the focus is formed, it is normal to feel confused, lost, and even worried; after the focus has been formed, you will probably feel relieved. You will have determined your goal, and you will have a greater sense of direction. The next task is that of collecting information. This task should be approached in a systematic, organized manner. You must become proficient in identifying, reading, and taking notes about the information you locate.

Thesis Statement

Now that your research has begun, you can draw some preliminary conclusion(s) based on the information you have gathered. This is called a *thesis statement*. You need a thesis statement to keep you on track. The thesis statement is the point you are going to discuss or prove in your paper. A thesis statement should act as mortar—holding together the various bricks of a paper, summarizing the main point of the paper, and guiding the paper's development. A thesis statement is an assertion, not a statement of fact, and often will be expressed in a sentence or two. Thesis statements take a stand, such as:

- The life of a teenager in the 1960s was very different from the lifestyle of most teenagers in the twenty-first century.

- Continuing changes in the Social Security System make it almost impossible to plan intelligently for retirement.
- The primary problem of the American steel industry is the lack of funds to renovate outdated plants and equipment.
- Because half of all crack babies are likely to grow up in homes without positive cognitive and emotional stimulation, the federal government should finance programs to supplement parental care for crack kids.
- Hunger persists in Appalachia because jobs are scarce and farming the infertile soil is rarely profitable.

A thesis is the main idea, not the title. It is narrow, not broad, specific, not general. A good thesis statement has one main point rather than several and typically features four attributes:

1. It addresses a subject about which reasonable people could disagree.
2. It deals with a subject that can be researched and described.
3. It expresses one main idea.
4. It asserts your conclusions about a subject.

Collecting Information

If your work is to be effective, you must make a series of crucial choices as you begin to collect information. First, it is important to consult a variety of resources. Each type of resource (e.g., a book or a journal) has its own attributes. These attributes are discussed in the next paragraph. Second, it is vital that you evaluate the information collected for accuracy and authority, bias, currency, and scope.

The most familiar information sources are books, journals, magazines, and newspapers. Books cover virtually every imaginable topic. Today books come in two formats: print and electronic. Journals (or magazines/periodicals) also come in both print and electronic formats (some are full-text, others merely abstracts). Journals are a good source for scholarly information—both current and historical. Often, editorial policy requires that other experts review journal articles for accuracy, writing style, etc. (referred to as "peer-reviewed journals"). Magazines are less academic. They typically contain popular culture issues, leisure reading, hobbies, and so on. Newspapers cover local, national, and worldwide current events, as well as other topics.

Today much information is retrieved from the Internet, an unorganized medium that varies greatly in quality. Enormous amounts of in-

Online Writing Resources

Merriam-Webster Dictionary

* http://m-w.com

Thesaurus.com

* www.thesaurus.com

The following Web sites will also assist you in learning to write:

Guide to Writing a Basic Essay

* http://members.tripod.com/~lklivingston/essay

Eleven Rules of Writing

* http://junketstudies.com/rulesofw/

The Nuts and Bolts of College Writing

* http://nutsandbolts.washcoll.edu

The Elements of Style

* www.bartleby.com/141

The Online English Grammar

* www.EduFind.com/english/grammar

Garbl's Writing Center

* http://garbl.home.attbi.com

EditAvenue.com

* www.editavenue.com

formation from Web sites, electronic journals, newspapers, and electronic books are available on the Internet—but not all of it is truthful, accurate, authoritative, current, or reliable. Because the Internet lacks organization, it can be quite difficult to locate the information you are seeking efficiently and effectively. All Internet (and other) information should be closely evaluated.

Learn to Be a "Good" Writer

Anyone can learn to write—and write well. It takes desire and determination. One of the most difficult tasks in writing is to begin. It is important to write down your thoughts and ideas—anything to get you started—and you can proceed from there. In addition, there are a few basic steps to assist you in the writing process:

1. *Identify and develop your topic.* Topic identification and development requires basic research of the idea you are considering.
2. *Locate background information.* Read about your topic. If you are conducting Internet research, look up keywords, and then synonyms of those keywords to narrow your search. It takes time to find just what you want. Remember, textbooks and other print sources are also useful for integrating information into your topic. (This will be further explored in Chapters 3 and 5.)
3. *Use the library.* Online databases and indexes are extremely helpful for locating recent articles on your topic. Learn how to access and use these databases and indexes appropriately. Remember, some online articles contain only abstracts (you must locate the journal), and some are full-text. (Chapter 4 will explain this in more detail.)
4. *Locate information on the Internet.* This is not always easy. Use search engines, subject directories, and the Invisible (or Deep) Web to locate materials efficiently on the Internet. (See Chapter 5.)
5. *Look for information in other formats.* Consider videotapes, CD-ROMs, DVDs, and audiotapes. These, too, are valuable for your research.
6. *Remember to evaluate everything you locate.* See Chapter 6 for how to evaluate information. It is a critical component of effective research.
7. *Cite what you find and where you found it.* In other words, write down where you located the information and all of the accompanying information (title, author, place of publication, publisher, publication date, which are all required information for the bibliography). (See Chapter 8 for citation styles and sources.)
8. *Work from the general to the specific.* Locate background information first, and then use more specific and recent resources.
9. *Do not forget the obvious help.* Use dictionaries and thesauri to assist you.

CONCLUSION

Learning the process of seeking information is as important as expanding your understanding of subject matter. Ideas lead to the need for further information, and this continues until the search is concluded. The process of information gathering can lead to your becoming information literate—and creating a successful research project. You must become conscious of your own thoughts and feelings as you progress through the research process. You will eventually become aware of how to systematically work though the stages of research and information access/literacy—lifelong learning. Remember that it is critical to consult a variety of resources before deciding on your precise research topic. You should not be solely dependent on one or two sources. It is also important to evaluate the information you locate. There is no doubt that there is an enormous amount of information from which to choose. Selecting and locating a research topic is your first large step in creating effective and relevant research.

REFERENCES AND FURTHER READING

Chapman, Linda, and Joanne Marien. 1999. "Research Skills 2000." *Instructor,* 109: 29–32.

Kranich, Nancy. 2001. "Libraries: Ensuring Information Equity in the Digital Age." *American Libraries,* 32: 7–8.

Kuhlthau, Carol Collier. 2000. *Teaching the Library Research Process: A Step-by-Step Program for Secondary Students.* West Nyack, NY: The Center for Applied Research in Education.

Milam, Peggy. 2002. *InfoQuest: A New Twist on Information Literacy.* Worthington, OH: Linworth.

Quaratiello, Arlene Rodda. 2000. *The College Student's Research Companion* (2nd ed.). New York: Neal-Schuman.

Slavens, Thomas P. 1994. *Sources for Historical Research.* New York: Neal-Schuman.

Whitley, Peggy, Catherine Olson, and Susan Goodwin. 2001. 99 *Jumpstarts to Research.* Greenwood Village, CO: Libraries Unlimited.

Yucht, Alice H. 1997. *FLIP IT! An Information Skills Strategy for Student Researchers.* Worthington, OH: Linworth.

Chapter 3

How Do I Find the Information I Need?

Searching is a creative process of discovery that can expand your knowledge and broaden your views. With the wealth of information available today, it is important to focus your search and reduce what you locate to a manageable amount. Searching is all about selecting the best resources and effective strategies, techniques, and tools.

PLANNING YOUR SEARCH

A Possible Search Plan

A library search takes time, interest, and a little of the detective's investigative instinct. It also requires the patience to stay with a task to its conclusion. There are numerous ways to plan a search for information, but you need a systematic approach. This is *one example* that includes some basic steps for success:

Step One: *Understand your research-assignment topic.* If it is not clear to you, ask your instructor. Look at some general resources that treat your topic to gain a better understanding of the area (for example, encyclopedias, dictionaries, handbooks, directories, etc.).

Step Two: *Create your search plan.* You need a plan to begin your search. Your search plan should contain keywords that describe the information you are seeking, along with information about the relationship between the keywords. It is wise to develop a minimum of two "concepts" that pertain to the topic along with appropriate keywords. For example, if your assignment is to research some aspect of the Underground Railroad, concept one could be a discussion of a major leader of the Underground Railroad, such as Harriet Tubman. Some possible keywords are Harriet Tubman, Underground Railroad, slavery, emancipation, Civil War, and so on. Concept two might be the role the Quakers played in the Underground Railroad. Some of the keywords for this concept might be Quakers, slaves, and abolitionists. By compiling a list of similar and related terms (synonyms—use a thesaurus), your chances of locating relevant information will greatly increase. To practice this step, complete Figure 3.1, Search Strategy (workform)

Search Strategy (workform)

		Please write a sentence describing your topic		
1	Search Question			
		List as many as needed		
2	Major Concepts	1. 2. 3.		
		Search Terms		
3	Concepts 1	and Concepts 2	and	Concepts 3
or				
or				
or				
or				
or				
or				
or				
or				
or				

Figure 3.1   Search Strategy (workform)

Step Three: *Decide on the types and formats of information sources you might need for your assignment.* You will need to select the types and formats of information sources that best meet the needs of the assignment.

Information types might include:

- historical,
- current,
- government,
- technical,
- statistical,
- research,
- legal, and
- demographic.

Information formats might include:

- books (print and electronic),
- journal articles (print and electronic),
- videos,
- charts,
- CD-ROMs,
- DVDs,
- newspapers,
- Web sites, and
- people (interviews).

Information is typically created in response to an event or phenomenon and is published in several different forms and sources. Sometimes the difference in information sources depends on how much time has elapsed between the event and publications about the event. For example, consider the Underground Railroad assignment. Ponder the time period of the Underground Railroad; approximately 1861–1867. From this information, you may determine that much of the information you need might come from print sources (because it is not a current topic), such as books, encyclopedias (print, CD-ROM, or online), videotapes, and perhaps some electronic or print journal articles and the Internet (however, these resources are less likely to include information necessary for the assignment).

Step Four: *Get ready to search by creating search statements.* A search statement is a set of instructions or a group of keywords that will help to locate appropriate information. For instance, for the Underground Railroad assignment, possible search statements might be "Harriet Tubman and Underground Railroad," or "Quakers and slavery," or "abolitionists and Underground Railroad."

Step Five: *Locate and obtain the information needed for your assignment.* Identify the type of reference—a book, book chapter, video, and journal article. Always write down the name, location, and all other pertinent data about the resource for use as a possible reference in your research paper.

Step Six: *Evaluate the information/resources you have gathered.* (Refer to Chapter 6 for detailed information regarding evaluation of print, nonprint, and electronic resources.)

A CLOSER LOOK AT SEARCH TOOLS

Finally, let's take a look at some possible resources in more depth.

- *Books.* Books are typically in print format, although more and more electronic books (e-texts) are becoming available. For the most part, books are written by experts and evaluated by a number of authoritative individuals before publication. Therefore, the information is typically accurate and reliable. However, books can become dated very quickly, particularly in areas such as the physical sciences, medicine, technology, or geography. There is a wide variety of reference books that are excellent for conducting research, ranging from atlases to handbooks to directories to dictionaries. Reference books are a good starting point to locate facts about a particular topic. Although books are useful, a combination of search tools and resources provides the most accurate and complete information.

- *Journals.* Journal articles are also typically written and reviewed by scholars. The information in journals can be extremely current and covers every imaginable subject. Scholarly articles tend to be viewed as credible and authoritative. Many journals can be accessed electronically via online databases (such as ProQuest, EBSCO, etc.). These online databases allow you to access numerous articles from a variety of journals, magazines, and newspapers. Companies (such as ProQuest) hire professionals to write this information and make it available for you via the Internet. Some databases, such as Academic Search Elite, Business Source Premier, and ScienceDirect, contain full-text articles and some merely provide abstracts.

- *Magazines.* Magazines are *generally* not considered scholarly and tend to cover popular culture and leisure reading on a wide variety of topics, from *Golf Digest* and *Popular Mechanics* to *Computer World* and *Road and Track*. The targeted audience of many magazines is the general public. Certain magazines are considered to be somewhat more scholarly than others, such as *Time*, *Newsweek*, *National Geographic*, and others. Some magazines, as with journals, are now in electronic format (e-journal or e-zine).

- *Newspapers.* Newspapers cover local, national, and international current events, as well as other subjects. Some newspapers are specific to a particular topic, such as the *Wall Street Journal*. Because many newspapers are published daily, they are extremely current, and a large number are available electronically.

- *Library Catalogs.* Library catalogs are a record of all of the materials that a particular library owns. They are organized and easily searchable. Most library catalogs are automated (electronic, called Online Public Access Catalogs or OPACs) and, in addition to author, title, subject, use keyword searching. (In keyword searching, the database software searches for the occurrence of the search term in one or more fields of each record, such as in the title or abstract.) Many library catalogs can be accessed from locations other than the library, for example, from your home computer or office.

- *Periodical Databases.* Periodical databases provide a searchable index to magazine, journal, and newspaper articles (either to abstracts or full-text articles). A periodical is any information that is issued regularly—daily, weekly, monthly, annually, etc. *Examples* of electronic databases are ProQuest, EBSCO, or CINAHL. (Note: periodical databases are the same as journal databases.)

- *The Internet.* The Internet is a network that connects computers worldwide, enabling people to communicate with each other and share information. (See Chapter 5.)

Exercise: Planning a Search

Try your hand at the "search plan" explained in this chapter. Choose an area that interests you (for example, Afghanistan, dyslexia, car racing, women in politics, etc.) and complete the worksheet in Figure 3.2. Sometimes, putting it in "black-and-white" is helpful. When ideas move from your mind to the page, they become more real and you remain more focused. Remember, effective searching begins with effective search strategies, which begin with clear and interesting questions. You may need to refer back to this chapter for assistance, but soon, this procedure should become easier and easier.

Planning a Search (worksheet)

STEPS	TASK	DESCRIPTION
1	Write down your research assigment specifically.	
2	Visit the library and view 3 general resources about your assigment/topic.	
3	Write 5 keyswords (remember to use a thesaurus!)	1. 2. 3. 4. 5.
4	Develop 2 concepts of the topic.	1. 2.
5	List the types and formats of materials you might need for your research.	
6	Create 2 search statements.	1. 2.
7	Locate resources (print, nonprint, online, people) appropriate for your research.	1. 2. 3. 4. 5.
8	Write down pertinent information about each of the 5 resources (where found, tittle, author or creator, publication date, place or publication, publisher, summary).	
9	Evaluate the 5 resources (refer to Chapter 6).	

Figure 3.2 Planning a Search (worksheet)

SEARCH TOOLS AND TECHNIQUES

Consider this scenario: All of the books, magazines, journals, and newspapers in your library (or home) are piled in a big heap on the floor. How would you find the specific information you need? Luckily, people have developed techniques and tools to make searching much easier for you. When using an electronic library catalog, you can search for materials by author, title, subject, keyword—a wide variety of methods. However, there are more advanced search strategies for locating information. Let's take a closer look at a variety of these search tools and techniques:

- *Boolean Logic.* This approach was originally developed in the mid-1800s by George Boole. It allows you to limit or broaden your search by using the connector words AND, OR, and NOT. Using AND or NOT between keywords will reduce the number of items found (however, they reduce results in different ways). For example, "Quakers AND Underground Railroad" will locate resources that could contain both terms: Quakers and Underground Railroad. "Quakers NOT Underground Railroad" will not locate information on the Underground Railroad as it relates to Quakers, but will find other materials on Quakers. Always remember that there is a possible loss of good information when using the Boolean operator NOT. Using OR between keywords will increase the number of results found. OR is best used with topics that do not retrieve many results. "Quakers OR Underground Railroad" will find resources that contain either the term Quakers or the term Underground Railroad. Figure 3.3 is a visual representation of Boolean Logic.

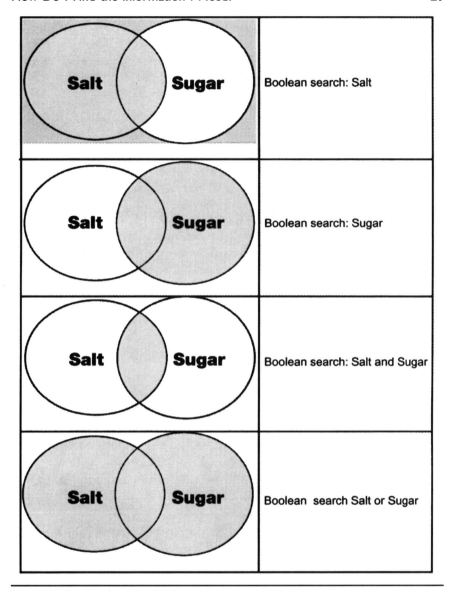

Figure 3.3   Boolean Logic Venn Diagram

Boolean Searching

For additional information regarding Boolean Searching, explore the following Web sites:

How Boolean Logic Works

www.howstuffworks.com/boolean1.htm

This Web site provides additional information regarding Boolean searching.

Boolean Searching

www.searchenginewatch.com/facts/boolean.html

Boolean Searching on the Internet

http://library.albany.edu/internet/boolean.html

This Web site is an easy-to-read and comprehensive guide to Boolean searching on Internet search engines.

- *Limiters.* Limiters can help you focus your topic and decrease the number of "hits" you will need to read through. Among the many limiters are material type, language, and date published. In other words, when conducting a search, you can specify video as the type of material, and the information retrieved will be in that format only. Another example is date of publication. You may select, for example, the year 2002. This will limit of your retrievals to information published only in the year 2002.
- *Truncation.* Truncation is helpful when searching for terms that could have several endings. An example of this search strategy is to type "educat*." With this truncated term, you will find information on education, educator, educate, or any word that begins "educat."
- *Phrase Searching.* This tool uses quotation marks to search for results that contain those words together rather than search for all instances of each separate word. For example, the phrase "sexually transmitted diseases" will locate information on diseases that are transmitted sexually.
- *Wildcards.* Wildcards can be helpful when you are unsure of the correct spelling of a word. A wildcard is the insertion of a question

mark symbol in place of a letter that you do not know. For example, "labo?r" will locate both the U.S. and British spellings of "labor/labour." Another example is "wom?n," which will capture irregular singular and plurals of "woman." Wildcards are sometimes called internal truncation or stemming.

- *Match-All Search.* This technique is similar to the Boolean tool AND, but it uses the symbol "+" rather than the word AND. For example, "Quakers + Underground Railroad" will provide information that pertains to both terms, "Quakers" and "Underground Railroad." Likewise, you may use the symbol "−" like the Boolean operator NOT. "Quakers − Underground Railroad" will locate information on Quakers but not on their connection to the Underground Railroad.
- *Title Searching.* Many of the major search engines and databases allow you to search with the HTML title of a Web page. This is the text that appears on the title page of a document. For example, a page may have an HTML title like this: <title>Harriet Tubman and the Underground Railroad<title>. If you know the title of the Web site or database, you can use it to proceed directly to that Web site or database.

By exploring search engines such as Google, AltaVista, and HotBot, you can determine which tools and techniques are specific to that particular one. The more experienced you become with effectively and efficiently using search tools and techniques, and the more familiar you become with a variety of search engines, the easier your research will be. Three tips to keep in mind while you are searching for information are:

Tip 1: Be sure that your search results ("hits") are relevant.
- Do they match up with the search terms you used?
- Do you need to use different search terms for this database?
- Do the references match the keywords but not the kind of information you need?
- Did you enter the search statement correctly and use the correct commands?
- Are you in the most appropriate database?

Tip 2: If you received too many references, you can:
- Add another concept to make it more specific (narrow your search).
- Make certain that you are using the Boolean operators correctly.

- Add limits to your search (for example, document type or particular years).

Tip 3: If your search did not yield enough references:
- Try searching a broader term.
- Make certain that you are using the Boolean operators correctly.
- Use alternative keywords (synonyms).
- Truncate search terms if needed.
- Try another database.

Exercise: Search Engines

Explore the following search engines and answer the listed questions about each. These three relatively popular search engines differ in various ways. It is helpful to learn about a variety of search engines because they perform different functions, use different methods of searching, and concentrate on different subjects. Note: some of this information may be located in the "help" section or under "advanced searching" in the search engine:

- Google   www.google.com
- AltaVista   www.altavista.com
- HotBot   www.hotbot.com

Questions

1. Does it use Boolean logic?
2. Can you use truncation?
3. Is phrase searching allowed?
4. Can you use wildcards?
5. What are the limiters available?

Ok, let's make this a bit more fun! Scenario: You are interested in finding out ways to submit a screenplay to a Hollywood studio...or you are interested in how to become a Hollywood movie producer (e.g., Do you need a degree? In what?). Use the three search engines above to locate information about one of the topics.

- Which search engine was more helpful?
- Which search engine gave you the most results?
- Which search engine provided the most relevant, useful cites?

(continued on next page)

Exercise: Search Engines (continued)
• Which search engine was most user-friendly (easier to navigate and understand)? • List one thing you liked and disliked about each search engine. • Did you find the answer to your question…which search engine provided it?

CONCLUSION

Effective research requires knowledge of various search tools and search techniques. Familiarity with them can make searching much more efficient and accurate. Always begin by searching a number of sources (e.g., books, online journals) and continue by using the techniques and tools explained in this chapter to locate precise information for your research project.

REFERENCES AND FURTHER READING

Allen, Bryce L. 2001. "Boolean Browsing in an Information System: An Experimental Test." *Information Technology and Libraries,* 20: 12–20.

Drabenstott, Karen M. 2001. "Web Search Strategy Development." *Online,* 25: 18–27.

Hock, Randolph. 2000. "Web Search Engines: (More) Features and Commands." *Online,* 24: 17–26.

McElmeer, Sharron L. 1999. "Kids Searching the WWW." *Book Report,* 18: 54.

Powell, William. 2002. "Bully Boolean." *Training and Development,* 56: 21–22.

Vine, Rita. 2001. "Real People Don't Do Boolean: How to Teach End Users to Find High-Quality Information on the Internet." *Information Outlook,* 5: 16–23.

Chapter 4

How Can the Library Help Me?

Both traditional and virtual (online) libraries contain vast amounts of organized information, from print books to online journal articles. Recently, there has been much speculation regarding the future existence of libraries. What is there to speculate about? Regardless of type, libraries offer structured access to practically everything you want to know and learn. Actually, libraries are more popular now than ever before. Pollsters estimate that as many as 80 percent of Americans use libraries every year. A virtual library is available electronically 24/7, typically easy to access, has evaluated information, and is well-organized. Libraries have a systematic way of cataloging (or arranging) information so you can locate your desired information. Libraries and librarians can assist you with your research in numerous ways—take advantage of these resources!

LIBRARY POLICIES AND SERVICES

It is common for a library's mission statement to read something like this: "The library will provide comprehensive information services to meet the curricular, research, cultural, and recreational needs of all users. This mission will be accomplished by providing:

- A rich variety of print, nonprint, and electronic materials and resources that enhance the curriculum as well as additional resources for personal improvement and recreation.
- Assistance and instruction in the use of information resources by a staff of trained professionals.
- A learning environment with services and equipment that facilitate the use of materials and resources."

To meet these requirements, libraries must write and uphold certain policies and procedures. These are critical documents to help ensure that libraries can operate efficiently and effectively. Typically, policies are defined as "why" documents; they provide a rationale for doing something. On the other hand, procedures tell you how to "do" something. Libraries have policies that cover areas such as circulation, access requirements, and Internet-use policies. These policies and procedures are for *your* benefit. They allow you such luxuries as the freedom to access appropriate, accurate, and current materials and equipment.

Visit Spalding University Online Library (*www.spalding.edu/library*) for an example of a library home page. Notice the "Online Reference" section. It allows you to pose reference questions via the Internet—a big help, right? Notice, too, that the online library provides subject Web links, such as nursing and education.

LIBRARY SERVICES

Libraries offer a wide variety of services, depending on the type and size of the library. The following are a few of the many services libraries provide.

- *Reserve Materials*. These are materials placed on reserve by an instructor for use by students in a specific class; they are typically held at the circulation desk in larger libraries.
- *Interlibrary Loans*. If you need materials such as books or copies of journal articles not available at that particular library, your library can borrow them from another library for your use.
- *Assistance (personal and/or online)*. Librarians provide numerous services to library users, such as basic research, evaluation of resources, citing resources, writing/research tools, and much more. Librarians can assist you with quick reference questions or with more detailed and involved issues. You can ask reference questions in person, by telephone, via e-mail, and even by chat reference—depending on the library. It is to your benefit to use the services of the reference librarian.
- *Online, Real-Time Reference Services*. This is a relatively new service in which students and librarians "co-browse" the reference materials together. If you are attending school, check out which virtual reference services are available.

It may be useful at this point to review how to look for resources in a traditional library. Materials are cataloged so you can locate them quickly and easily. Libraries use two major classification systems: Library of Congress (LC) and Dewey Decimal Classification (DDC) systems. Most small and school libraries use Dewey Decimal; most academic and larger public libraries use the Library of Congress Classification System. Regardless of the classification system employed, you can enter keywords (such as author, title, subject) into the online catalog to locate the particular items (arranged on the shelf by call number). It is helpful to practice locating sources in your library using their classification system. For the Dewey Decimal Classification system, visit Let's Do Dewey at *www.mtsu.edu/~vvesper/dewey.html*

How Libraries Work

It's good to understand how libraries work because they can be your best friends while you are conducting research. We are fortunate to live in a country that allows us access to many, many types of information. This is not the case everywhere in the world. Do you know what rights you have as a library user?

LIBRARY ONLINE ASSISTANCE

Many libraries offer online assistance through the online library catalog, indexes, databases, and other Web links. A library's online public access catalog (OPAC) can typically be searched in a variety of methods: title keyword, author keyword, subject keyword, general keyword, series keyword, journal keyword, title browse, author browse, series browse, subject browse, and journal browse are common methods. This makes locating materials more efficient and effective. Periodical indexes and databases allow you to search for citations to articles in popular magazines, scholarly journals, newspapers, and dissertations and retrieve the full-text of articles or abstracts depending on the database. Often these indexes and databases are available both in the library and from a remote location, such as your home or a computer lab. Usually, to logon to the databases from outside of the library you need a special user identification (ID) and a password (available from that library). The sources listed on pages 39–41 are examples of online indexes and databases that may be found in a library. Your library may have some of these or others not listed. (Note: database providers such as EBSCO, FirstSearch, or ProQuest offer a variety of specific online databases. The providers for these examples are in parentheses.)

Exercise: Library Rights

Did you know that, "materials should not be excluded because of the origin, background, or views of those contributing to their creation"?

The next time you are in front of a computer, explore the following Web sites (produced by the American Library Association). You may learn something new and interesting!

The American Library Association Library Bill of Rights

www.ala.org/work/freedom/lbr.html

Code of Ethics of the American Library Association

Did you know that "they uphold the principles of intellectual freedom and resist all efforts to censor library resources"?

www.ala.org/alaorg/oif/ethics.html

Did you know that, "freedom to read is essential to our democracy...and it is continuously under attack"?

The Freedom to Read Statement

www.ala.org/alaorg/oif/freeread.html

These Web sites display the importance of libraries in the United States—they tell you what you are allowed to do because you live in a free country.

Did you realize how much your freedom to learn is being protected in the United States?

Do you disagree with any of these policies?

Do you think there is information that one should not be allowed to read?

After viewing these Web sites, select a controversial issue and debate it with a classmate. For instance, debate this issue with a friend: "Libraries should cooperate with all persons and groups concerned with resisting abridgment of free expression and free access to ideas." What is your point of view on this issue?

Academic Search Premier (via EBSCO): Searches over 3,000 scholarly journals, magazines, and trade publications from all academic disciplines.

AGRICOLA (via FirstSearch): Searches agriculture, forestry, and animal-science materials.

Alt-Health Watch (via EBSCO): Provides articles on alternative approaches to health care and wellness.

Alternative Press Index (via FirstSearch): Indexes approximately 300 journals covering cultural, economic, political, and social change.

ArtAbstracts (via FirstSearch): Indexes articles from the world's leading arts and humanities journals.

BioDigest (via FirstSearch): Provides life-science information in lay terms.

Biography Index (via FirstSearch): Contains full-text biography resources—articles, biographies, and Web sites.

Book Review Digest (via FirstSearch): Provides abstracted reviews of fiction and nonfiction works.

BooksInPrint (via FirstSearch): Provides information and reviews for in-print, out-of-print, and forthcoming books.

Business Source Elite (via EBSCO): Provides full-text for over 1,000 business journals, magazines, and trade publications for news and events.

Business Wire News (via EBSCO): Contains a collection of full-text newswires covering news from all over the world about business, political, economic, and international news events.

Chronicle of Higher Education (via Chronicle): Provides full coverage of the *Chronicle of Higher Education*.

CINAHL (via FirstSearch): Contains a cumulated index of nursing and allied health literature.

Consumers Index (via FirstSearch): Indexes numerous articles providing consumer information.

DataTimes (via FirstSearch): Provides an index of United States, international, and regional newspapers.

Dissertation Abstracts (via FirstSearch): Contains abstracts of dissertations from all over the world.

Education Abstracts (via FirstSearch): Includes leading publications in the field of education.

ERIC (via FirstSearch): Contains abstracts of documents and journal articles on educational research and practice.

FactSearch (via FirstSearch): Includes facts and statistics on topics of current interest.

Facts.com (via Facts.com): Provides full-text national and international current events information.

GEOBASE (via FirstSearch): Contains worldwide literature on geography, geology, and ecology.

Government Printing Office (via FirstSearch): Contains information concerning United States government publications.

Grove's Dictionary of Art Online (via Groveart.com): This is the most comprehensive online reference resource for all aspects of the visual arts worldwide—prehistory to the present day, including relevant articles, images, and Web sites.

Literature Resource Center (via Gale): Provides full-text resources with access to biographies, bibliographies, and critical essays of authors from every age and literary discipline.

MEDLINE (via FirstSearch): Contains abstracted articles from several thousand medical journals.

Reader's Guide Abstracts (via FirstSearch): Contains abstracts of articles from popular magazines.

SIRS Government Reporter (via SIRS): Provides full-text reports and information by and about the United States government.

SIRS Renaissance (via SIRS): Contains information regarding arts and humanities with full-text.

SIRS Researcher (via SIRS): Provides articles on social, scientific, economic, and political issues worldwide.

WilsonSelectPlus (via FirstSearch): Contains full-text articles in science, humanities, education, and business.

WorldAlmanac (via FirstSearch): Contains world facts and statistics.

WorldBook (via FirstSearch): The World Book Encyclopedia.

Databases contain an enormous amount of information that may be useful for your research. Current journal and newspaper articles include relevant, specialized, and important information. Each database serves a different purpose and population. For example, the ERIC database locates information (primarily) about education. The CINAHL database provides articles and abstracts that deal with nursing and health issues. By learning about various databases that your library holds, you can research more effectively and efficiently.

Exercise: Indexes and Databases
Visit your local public, school, or academic library. This may take a bit of time, but it is well worth the effort. Each library purchases specific indexes and databases. What they buy depends on the size of the library, the type of library, and what the librarian selects. It is a good idea to talk to your librarian about the indexes and databases available in your library, and acquire any other information you can from him/her. Then access a variety of the online indexes and databases that your library has available and complete the worksheet in Figure 4.1. What is the purpose of this task? Just as you learn more about driving a car by doing it than reading about it, it is much easier to learn about indexes and databases if you explore and use them.
List the databases you accessed. What is their primary focus (area, subject)? Are they useful (contain lots of pertinent articles) and user-friendly (easy to maneuver around in)? The worksheet provided will be helpful in reminding you of which indexes and databases are of importance for your research; which ones cover what topics (subject areas); which ones are easy to operate. Which database did you rate the highest? Why?

1	What subject areas does it Includes?	
2	Does it offer full text articles?	Yes No
3	Can you search by:	1. Author 2. Title 3. Keyword
4	Does it include an advanced search?	Yes No
5	Can you print the information?	Yes No
6	Will it sort for you?	1. By date 2. Relevance
7	Can you print the information?	Yes No
8	Can you send the information to your email address?	Yes No
9	Does it tell you the number of "hits" found?	Yes No
10	Does it provide a search history?	Yes No
11	Does it include a "help" component?	Yes No
12	It is user-friendly/easy to access and use?	Yes No
13	How do you rate this database?	From 1 2 3 4 5 6 7 8 9 10

Figure 4.1   Online Database (worksheet).

VIRTUAL LIBRARIES

What are virtual libraries? Virtual libraries are a managed collection of information resources and services available electronically through the Internet. Virtual libraries provide databases, indexes, online library catalogs (from a variety of libraries), interlibrary loans, government information, and numerous services (including virtual reference desks)—all available online. Many states now have their own online libraries; these are your gateways to information and research assistance. Virtual libraries provide high-quality research and complex search services—they are organized information (libraries) through the Internet. However, it is important to understand that virtual libraries cannot perform *all* of the functions of an "actual library." They do not yet offer personal assistance, or activities and services for learning and enjoyment.

Virtual Libraries

For additional information regarding virtual libraries, visit the following Web sites (You might also contact your local library regarding your state's virtual library):

Education Virtual Library

www.csu.edu.au/education/library.html

This Web site provides information via a virtual university from Charles Sturt University.

The WWW Virtual Library

www.vlib.org

This site includes areas to research from "agriculture" to "society." Note: numerous extremely specialized virtual libraries exist, as well as general virtual libraries.

ERAU Virtual Library

www.embryriddle.edu/libraries/virtual

This Web site from the Embry Riddle Aeronautical University provides 1,911 links regarding aerospace and aviation.

CONCLUSION

Libraries are systematic. They provide organized information—print, nonprint, and electronic. Libraries and librarians are your answer to research. Whether traditional or virtual, libraries allow you to locate information from a multitude of sources. Become friends with your librarian.

REFERENCES AND FURTHER READING

Bolger, Dorita F. 2000. "Evolving Virtual Library II: Practical and Philosophical Perspectives." *Journal of Interlibrary Loan, Document Delivery and Information Supply,* 11: 127–129.

D'Angelo, Barbara J. 2001. "What Is a Virtual Library?" *Library Technology Reports,* 37: 5–8.

Steele, Noreen O. 2000. "Success Factors for Virtual Libraries." *E-Content,* 23: 68–71.

"Vast Reaches." *American Libraries,* 32: 40–45.

Williams, Wilda W. 2002. "Planning for Library Services to People with Disabilities." *Library Journal,* 127: 148–156.

Chapter 5

There Is So Much Information on the Internet. Where Do I Begin?

(A glossary of terms used in this chapter is located at the end of this chapter. A glossary of all terms used in this book is located at the end of this book.)

Knowing how to describe what you are looking for, deciding where the best places are to begin looking, and being able to evaluate a source's authority are critical to research in today's world. As a student, you must become familiar with the Internet and know how to navigate it to become a successful learner. In the twenty-first century, it is up to you to learn how to research—to become information literate—to *learn to learn.*

THE INTERNET

The Internet has been in existence—changing and growing—for over 30 years. It is a network of networks, linking computers to computers. The Internet is the transport vehicle for the information stored in files or documents on other computers. It is a massive network that consists of interconnected sub-networks worldwide. (Note: The Internet itself does not contain information. Rather than saying that a document was "found on the Internet," it would be more accurate to say that it was found "through or using" the Internet.) The Internet consists of an enormity of unorganized information. No one individual or group manages or owns it; it is a self-publishing medium. The Internet is a bulletin board containing everything from the authentic to the unauthentic. Today, the Internet is changing at staggering rates and is becoming more readily available to everyone. No one actually knows what the long-term impact of the Internet will be.

The Internet is comprised of the World Wide Web and various text-only resources, which presents information in text, graphic, video, and audio formats. The World Wide Web is estimated to contain approximately four billion documents. When you "search" the Web, you are not actually searching it directly. The Web is the totality of the many Web "pages" that reside on computers all over the world. Your computer cannot locate or retrieve them all directly. What you are able to do through your computer is access one or more of the many intermediate search tools now available. You explore a search tool's database or collection of sites—a relatively small subset of the entire World Wide Web. When you access the Internet using a browser, you are viewing documents on the World Wide Web.

- A browser is a computer program (a software application, such as Netscape or Internet Explorer) that resides on your computer, enabling you to use the computer to view World Wide Web documents—to locate and display Web pages. Browsers allow you to click on hypertext links (with URLs to other pages) to retrieve information via the Web, and offer additional features for navigating and managing the Web.
- A URL (Universal Resource Locator) is the most basic information about where a Web page is located on the World Wide Web. It includes information about which Web server the page is stored, in which directory it is located, its name, and the protocol used to retrieve it. The following is an example of what a URL looks like: *http://www.m-w.com/dictionary.htm*, which is the *Merriam Webster Dictionary* online.

  - The "http" is the protocol; the *"m-w.com"* is the domain.
  - "dictionary.htm" is the directory or file.
  - The three-letter suffix on the end of the domain name is perhaps the most revealing part of a URL. Currently, there are six common domains. The six domains presently in use are:
    - com (commercial)
    - org (organization)
    - net (business)
    - gov (government)
    - mil (military)
    - edu (education).
  However, seven new domains are presently being developed.
    - aero (Air-Transport Industry)

- biz (business)
- coop (cooperatives)
- info (unrestricted)
- museum (museums)
- name (for registration by individuals),
- pro (accountants, lawyers, and physicians).

Once a domain name is properly registered, no other person or company can use the same name. On the World Wide Web, the HTML allows a text area, image, or other object to become a chain or link that retrieves another computer file on the Internet. *HTML* stands for Hypertext Markup Language. It is a standardized language of computer code, containing the textual content, images, and links to other documents.

Searching the Internet successfully requires expertise. To find reliable, accurate information on the Internet and to navigate it efficiently and effectively, you must learn how it functions. It is important to remember that the Internet emphasizes quantity, not necessarily quality. It is an excellent tool for locating information, but it is typically not the best place to begin academic research. The World Wide Web is not indexed using any standard vocabulary. In Web searching, you are always guessing what words will be in the pages you want to find or speculating about the subject terms that someone may have chosen to organize a Web page or site covering a specific topic. This is the direct opposite of the organized system of an online public access catalog in your local library, which uses standard vocabulary and is much easier to search.

This Web site can be helpful for learning the basics of the Internet:

Beginner's Central, a User's Guide to the Internet
http://northernwebs.com/bc

Searching Efficiently and Effectively

The only easy and certain way to find the location of information on the Internet is to already know where it exists. This is difficult, however, because there is no complete index to the resources available on the Internet. Everything, *everything*, on the Internet must be analyzed for its appropriateness for research use (Chapter 6 explains this thoroughly). Sometimes finding Web documents or sites can be fairly simple, other times it seems impossibly difficult. This is partly because of its sheer size, but it is also because it is not indexed like a library's catalog. Actually, no one knows how many individual files reside on the Internet. In order to conduct research on the Internet, you must understand a variety of search tools that will assist you in finding the information desired.

There are three basic types of search tools: 1) search engines, 2) subject directories, and 3) the "Deep (or Invisible)" Web. These tools can unearth the vast resources of the Internet. It is vital to pick the right starting place, that is, the right search tools, as it will result in a more targeted result. Note the following five concerns before conducting your search:

- Many people use search engines without considering the usefulness of subject directories (discussed later in this chapter) for their topics.
- The difference between the three types of tools is often poorly understood.
- The Deep or Invisible Web (explained later in this chapter) is growing at a phenomenal rate, so its content is becoming increasingly important to researchers.
- All of these tools complement each other in the research process.
- The lines are blurring between sites that offer either one resource or another (for example, it is common to find directories and specialized searches on the Deep Web at many search engine sites).

Prior to beginning the research process, it is important to review the information discussed in Chapters 2 and 3 concerning subject and topic selection, as well as search strategies and techniques. You will find it necessary to explore multiple sites when you are investigating a topic. Search engines and subject directories vary in their contents, features, selectivity, accuracy, and retrieval technologies. In addition, the world of subject directories and search engines is a highly volatile one. Do not be dismayed if you visit a site and discover that things have changed. This is par for the course. Many of these sites are commercial enterprises and competition is keen. When changes occur, they are often for the better, as the service attempts to keep ahead of the pack. How do you actually locate information on the Internet? The following are some possible methods:

- Go directly to the site if you have the address (URL).
- Browse.
- Explore a subject directory.
- Conduct a search using a Web search engine.
- Explore the information stored in live databases on the Web (Deep or Invisible Web).

It critical that you view numerous sites when researching a topic using the Internet. Do not rely on only one Web site or one type of site.

SEARCH ENGINES

There is no way for anyone to search the entire Web, and any search tool that claims that it offers it all to you is distorting the truth. That being understood, one way to locate information on the Internet is to use a search engine. Search engines are a searchable database of Internet files collected by a computer program. The indexing is created from the collected files (e.g., title, full-text, size, etc.). There is no selection criteria for the files themselves although evaluation can be applied to the ranking. A search engine allows you to enter keywords relating to the topic and retrieve information about Internet sites containing those keywords. Remember that all search engines have rules for formulating queries. Read the "help files" at each site before proceeding. To practice this, look at the following search engines and determine their specific rules (remember to look for Help on the home page):

HotBot
www.hotbot.com

AltaVista
www.altavista.com

Directories (discussed in detail later in this chapter), such as Yahoo!, are designed for identifying general information. Similar to a library catalog, they classify Web sites into similar categories, such as natural history museums, accounting firms, etc. The results of your search will be a list of Web sites related to your specific search term. For instance, if you are looking for the Louvre Web site, use a directory. However, what if you want more specific information, such as biographical information about Leonardo da Vinci? Web indexes are the way to go, because they search the entire contents of a Web site. Indexes use software programs (called spiders and robots) that scour the Internet, analyzing millions of Web pages and indexing all of the words. Indexes such as Google and AltaVista find individual pages of a Web site that match your search criteria, even if the site itself has nothing to do with what you are looking for. Be prepared to wade through enormous amounts of irrelevant information when searching indexes.

Search engines do not search the Internet itself. They search databases of information about the Internet that the company hosting the search engine has developed. Each search engine looks through a different database. That is why you retrieve different sites from exactly the same terms (keywords) in different search engines. For targeted, complex, and sometimes-general queries, use a search engine. There are at least two ways a search engine finds out about a document and enters it into its database. One way is for the publisher of the document to register it with the search engine. The second is for the search engine company to find it as part of its research routines. (Note: Some pages and links are excluded from most search engines. This will be discussed later in this chapter.) Most search engines provide easy-to-use forms on which you enter keywords or phrases. Subject categories help you narrow your search terms and strategies, and advanced searching capabilities increase the chances of a more relevant list. There are numerous search engines and each one differs greatly.

You can receive better results from an Internet search engine if you know when to use it. So, when should you use a search engine? Use a search engine:

- when you have a narrow or obscure topic or idea to research;
- when you are looking for a specific site;
- when you want to retrieve a large number of documents on your topic;
- when you want to search for particular types of documents, file types, source locations, languages, date last modified, etc; or
- when you want to take advantage of newer retrieval technologies, such as concept clustering, ranking by popularity, link ranking, etc.

A meta-search engine is a search tool that does not create its own database of information, but instead searches those of other search engines. Metacrawler is a good example. It searches the databases of Lycos, WebCrawler, Excite, AltaVista, and Yahoo! Meta-search engines quickly and superficially search several individual search engines at once and return results compiled into a sometimes-convenient format. However, they only catch about 10 percent of the search results in any of the search engines they visit.

Every person searches for information differently and has favorite resources, whether they are print, nonprint, or Web sites. Good searching begins well before you enter the topic terms into a search engine. Critical thinking capabilities are as necessary in using a search engine as they are in using any print resource or database. Searching the Internet requires part skill, part luck, and a little bit of art.

Two useful Web sites dealing with search engines are listed in the box below. Take time to explore them.

Search Engines

Search Engine Watch

www.searchenginewatch.com

This site provides a wealth of useful information, such as "Web Searching Tips," Search Engine Listings," and "Search Engine Resources."

Search Engines:

What They Are, How They Work, and Practical Suggestions for Getting the Most Out of Them

http://webreference.com/content/search

This site provides background, how search engines work, and search examples.

In order to determine which search engines you prefer, you should explore a wide variety of them. You have previously viewed Google, HotBot, and AltaVista. Now let's explore a few more search engines. Think of the following questions while viewing them (see next page). Why are these search engines different from the ones you already explored? Because they offer different information, different types of searching, different subject material … they will broaden your horizons just a little more—dig in!

Exercise: Search Engines

Ask the following questions as you explore the three search engines listed below.

- Does it include links to detailed help?
- How large is it?
- What type of searching does it use (Boolean, phrase, etc.)?
- How does it search proper names?
- Does it have advanced searching?
- Is it case sensitive?

Dogpile

www.dogpile.com

Ask Jeeves

www.askjeeves.com

Lycos

www.lycos.com

Which one do you like best? Why? Which one do you like least? Why?

SUBJECT DIRECTORIES

Subject directories are subject "trees" that catalog or create classification schema for selected Web sites, organizing Internet sites by subject. Researchers who are starting with broad topics use directories to move from general information to more specific subsets of the information by accessing sub-folders within the classification schema. Unlike search engines, which perform keyword searches that are created by specific software programs, subject directories are built by humans (hand-selected and evaluated carefully); not computer programs. If you want to view Web sites that experts in a particular field recommend, use a subject directory. This allows you to choose a subject of interest and then browse the list of resources in that category. You conduct your search by selecting a series of progressively narrower search terms from a number of lists of descriptors provided in the directory. It is important to understand that a subject directory will not have links to every piece of information on the Internet, and they are much smaller than search-engine databases. Each subject directory has unique content and a unique emphasis. They are most useful when you are trying to narrow your topic, have a broad idea to research, or want to see a list of sites recommended by experts. Two general subject directories are Yahoo! and Librarians' Index to the Internet.

- *Yahoo!:* This commercial portal is the largest and most famous around. It provides limited descriptions and annotations, uses phrase searching ("") and allows subject searching.
- *Librarians' Index to the Internet:* This directory includes over 8,000 entries. It is compiled by library experts and uses highest quality sites only. It offers good and reliable annotations and allows Boolean searching.

There are some important points to keep in mind when using subject directories.

- There are two basic kinds of directories, academic /professional and commercial. Academic and professional directories are created and maintained by subject experts to support the needs of researchers. Commercial portals cater to the general public and are competing for traffic. Be sure you use the directory that appropriately meets your needs.
- Subject directories differ significantly in selectivity. Consider the policies of any directory that you visit.
- Many people do not make enough use of subject directories. Instead, they go straight to search engines. Keep in mind that academic subject directories contain carefully chosen and annotated lists of quality Internet sites.

When should you use a subject directory? Use a subject directory:

- when you have a broad topic or idea to research;
- when you want to see a list of Web sites on your topic that experts have recommended and annotated;
- when you want to retrieve a list of sites relevant to your topic rather than numerous individual pages contained within these sites;
- when you want to search for the site title, annotation, and (if available) assigned keywords to retrieve relevant material rather than the full-text document; or
- when you want to avoid viewing low-content documents that often turn up on search engines.

Which is better, search engines or subject directories? That depends on your personal preferences. Some people like subject directories because they can control the search pattern. Directories also allow you to browse and to be more general with your search terms. Search engines leave the searching pattern to the computer program and can be used to locate resources that are more specific. One weakness of subject directories is that you must depend on the descriptors provided by the company. A weakness of search engines is the extremely extensive amount of "hits" they can produce.

Exercise: Subject Directories

In order to understand subject directories more thoroughly, let's visit a few. This will allow you to decide if you prefer subject directories or search engines—or *both*, for their specific assistance. While you are visiting these sites, think of the following:

1. Do the annotations provide sufficient information?
2. Does it contain any full-text resources?
3. What type of searching does it use (phrase, Boolean, etc.)?
4. Is it user-friendly?

Yahoo!

www.yahoo.com

Yahoo! is the original search directory. You can go from broader topics to narrower ones.

Librarians' Index to the Internet

www.lii.org

This is a subject directory compiled by public librarians in the information supply business. It is of high quality and has reliable, useful annotations.

Do you see the difference between search engines and subject directories? Write down how you would describe the difference to a friend. Now, list three ways you would use a subject directory in your research paper:

1. _____

(continued on next page)

Exercise: Subject Directories *(continued)*

2. _____

3. _____

Ok, here are some more subject directories to explore:

Infomine

   http://infomine.ucr.edu

Academic Info

   www.academicinfo.net

THE DEEP WEB

The concept of the "Deep" or "Invisible" Web has recently emerged. This refers to content that is stored in databases accessible on the Web, but not available via search engines. In other words, this content is invisible to search engines because spiders or robots cannot or will not enter into databases and extract content from them as they can from static Web pages. The only way to access information on the Deep Web is to search the databases themselves. Topical coverage runs the gamut from scholarly resources to commercial entities. Very current, dynamically changing information is likely to be stored in databases, including news, job listings, airline flights, etc. As the number of Web-accessible databases grow, it will be essential to use them to conduct successful research on the Web.

When dealing with the Deep Web, keep the following in mind:

- Many databases on the Web are searchable from their own sites. Therefore, a good directory will link to these sites.
- There are Web sites that specialize in collecting links to databases available on the Web. One such site is actually called *The Invisible Web* (*www.invisibleweb.com*). This site links to approximately 10,000 Web-accessible databases.
- Topical coverage on the Deep Web is extremely varied. This presents a challenge, since it is impossible to anticipate what might turn up in a database. In addition, because databases proliferate on the Web the coverage will be fluid.

- Information that is dynamically changing in content will appear on the Deep Web. Examples are news, job postings, etc.
- Directories are a part of the Deep Web. A few examples are phone books and other "people finders"; lists of professionals, such as doctors and lawyers; patents; and dictionary definitions.

When should you use the Deep Web? Use the Deep Web:

- when you want dynamically changing content, or
- when you want to find information that is normally stored in a database, such as a phone book listing, geographical data, etc.

Do you understand the concept of the Deep or Invisible Web now? Ok, let's review. There are basically three ways to access information on the Internet (basically!): search engines, like AskJeeves; subject directories, like Yahoo!; and the Deep or Invisible Web, like the Web site ProFusion. The Deep Web contains information that you cannot find on either a search engine or a subject directory. Sounds mysterious, but if you look at the site ProFusion (*www.profusion.com*), it will become clearer.

Deep or Invisible Web Sites

For more examples of the Deep Web, visit the following sites:

Invisibleweb.com

www.invisibleweb.com

This is a directory of high quality databases on the Web that are especially useful to researchers.

WebData

www.webdata.com

This site offers a collection of searchable databases on the Web, organized into topics and maintained by ExperTelligence, Inc.

Exercise: The Internet

The following tutorial, from the University at Albany Libraries, will increase your knowledge of the Internet—what it is and how it works. You will discover several terms or phrases throughout this Web site that may be unfamiliar to you. However, the more Internet terminology you learn, the better the research you can conduct. Not only that, but you can impress your friends with your large, technological vocabulary. Locate the following terms within this Web site and provide their definitions:

University at Albany Libraries Internet Tutorials © 2002 Laura Cohen. Reproduced by permission.

http://library.albany.edu/internet

1. Telnet: _____
2. FTP: _____
3. E-mail discussion groups: _____
4. Usenet News: _____
5. Instant messaging: _____
6. MUD: _____
7. Ethernet: _____
8. Menu bar: _____
9. Service provider: _____

Now, let's do something more exciting. This Web site also contains an enormous amount of great information and many awesome links. Check out "How to Choose a Search Engine or Directory." Now, go to a search engine that provides "images" (you'll understand when you get there). Put in the word "animal"—pretty cool, huh? This time go to the Deep Web site Profusion and type in "Matt Damon"…then "Celine Dion." I'll bet you didn't know these were available on the Internet! List three new things that you learned by exploring this site.

1. _____
2. _____
3. _____

CONCLUSION

The Internet is a worldwide computer network that has forever changed the way people receive and transmit information. Its global nature facilitates communication among people of all nationalities in every country on the planet. Everyone is a potential message receiver and provider in this two-way communication system. As wonderful as the Internet is in providing an unbelievable wealth of information, it can also be an electronic nightmare for those who do not know how to use it properly. Three ways to more efficiently sift through the masses of information are 1) search engines, 2) subject directories, and 3) the Deep or Invisible Web. These tools assist in alleviating the potential thousands and thousands of hits one might receive using any one search term or phrase. These tools make Internet searching easier, more efficient, and more effective for your specific research.

REFERENCES AND FURTHER READING

Bruce, Christine. 1997. *Seven Faces of Information Literacy*. South Australia: AUSLIB Press.

Fialkoff, Francine. 2001. "Educate the Educators." *Library Journal*, 126: 2–4.

Jasco, Peter. 2002. "Northern Light Still Shine On." *Information Today*, 19: 30.

Levy, Steven. 2002. "Faster Than the Rest." *Newsweek*, 139 (25 March): 48.

McKenzie, Jamie. 1996. "Grazing the Net." *Phi Delta Kappan*, 80: 26–31.

Mitchoff, Kate Houston. 2002. "Explorers." *Library Journal*, 127: 37.

Notess, Greg R. 2002. "Internet Search Engine Update." *Online*, 26: 20.

Sherman, Chris and Gary Price. 2001. *The Invisible Web: Uncovering Information Sources Search Engines Can't See*. Medford, NJ: CyberAge Books.

Talbot, Dixie. 1997. "Search Engines Become Another Unit in Library Skills." *Book Report*, 16: 18–20.

Valenza, Joyce Kasman. 1997. "Master the Art of Searching." *Electronic Learning*, 16: 62.

GLOSSARY OF TERMS USED IN THIS CHAPTER

Boolean Logic: A way to combine terms using "operators" such as "AND" "OR" and "NOT." AND requires that all terms appear in a record. OR retrieves records with either term. NOT excludes terms.

Browser: This is a software program that enables you to view World Wide Web documents. They "translate" HTML-encoded files into the text, images, sounds, and other features you see. Examples are Netscape and Internet Explorer.

Directory: A system that your computer uses to organize files on the basis of specific information. Directories can be organized hierarchically so that files appear in a number of different ways, such as the order in which they were created, alphabetically by name or by type, and other ways.

Domain: A hierarchical scheme for indicating logical and sometimes geographical venues of a Web page from the network. Two examples are .edu (education) and .com (commercial).

HTML: Hypertext Markup Language. This is a standardized language of computer code, imbedded in "source" documents behind all Web documents. They contain the textual content, images, links to other documents, and formatting instructions for display on the screen.

Hypertext: A feature on the World Wide Web that allows a text area, image, or other object to become a "link" (like a chain) to retrieve other computer files on the Internet.

Link: The URL imbedded in another document, so that if you click on the highlighted text or button referring to the link, you retrieve the URL.

Meta-Search Engine: Search engines that automatically submit your keyword search to several other search tools and retrieve results from all of their databases.

Phrase Searching: A type of search that uses more than one keyword and is enclosed in quotation marks (" "). Sometimes called a character string.

Protocol: The standard or set of rules that two computers use to communicate with each other. Also known as a communications protocol or network protocol, this set of standards assures that different network products or programs can work together. Any product that uses a given protocol should work with any other product using the same protocol.

Robot: A program designed to automatically go out and explore the Internet for a specific purpose. Robots that record and index all of the contents of the network to create searchable databases are sometimes called *spiders*. WebCrawler and Lycos are examples of robots.

URL (Universal Resource Locator): The most basic information about where a page is located on the Internet. A URL can be used to directly access that site. It includes information about what server the page is stored in, in which directory it is located, its name, and the protocol used to retrieve it.

Chapter 6

How Do I Know If What I Read Is the Truth?

Print, nonprint, and Web-based resources offer you the opportunity to locate information and data from all over the world. However, finding appropriate, thought-provoking materials for academic research requires time and expertise. It is vital to evaluate all sources, identifying the most suitable ones for your research topic.

WHY EVALUATION IS IMPORTANT

Why is it necessary to evaluate the information you read? In the past, much of this evaluation was already taken care of for you. Publishers of books and other print items—at least those in established publishing houses—went to great lengths to ensure that the information was accurate, authoritative, and objective. Prior to publication of a print resource, experts in a given field evaluated the authors or creators of the work and their reputations. Scholarly works were evaluated by experts in the field for accuracy. In other words, much of the "evaluative work" was done before you even saw the publication. Today, with the immeasurable amount of information located on the Internet—and other sources, such as videotapes, CD-ROMs, DVDs, and various nonprint media—evaluation by the reader has become even more crucial. Remember, literally anyone can place information on the Internet. Therefore, it is up to you to ascertain if the information is accurate, objective, current, and useful.

Today there is a myriad of information and resources available via the Internet. This is good news and bad news. The good news is that so much more information is readily accessible, and the bad news is that much more of it is inadequate. Thus, it is your responsibility to develop expertise in evaluating the information you require.

Fortunately, evaluation is something that you all do almost on a daily basis without even realizing it. For example, when you watch a television program, don't you evaluate it (even if only in your own mind)? What about a new restaurant? Sometimes you evaluate things in your daily lives in a more formal way. For instance, you probably research a variety of cars before purchasing one. This same evaluation procedure is also important when conducting academic research; it helps you develop a high-quality product. For this reason, evaluation of print, nonprint, and Internet information is an extremely important aspect of research—and *learning to learn*.

FOUR KEY CRITERIA FOR EVALUATING INFORMATION

Specific criteria can assist you with the evaluation of resources—and make it easier for you to choose the "best" ones for your specific needs. There are four criteria you can use to evaluate information. Each one helps you to examine a different aspect of the work. These criteria are accuracy and authority, objectivity, currency, and scope.

Accuracy and Authority

The first step is to determine the accuracy and authority of your source. Indicators of authority include the education and experience of the authors, editors, and contributors, as well as the reputation of the publisher or sponsoring agency. Evaluating print resources is considerably easier than evaluating nonprint and Web-based materials. Why? Because in print publications much of the information needed for evaluation is provided in an easy-to-locate and easy-to-read manner. Let's consider a reference book (for example, a handbook). Who are the authors, editors, contributors, and publishers of the source? What credentials do they have and what kind of reputations? What else have they created? The answers to these questions are usually straightforward, because statements of authorship can usually be found on the title page and verso (back) of the title page. Typically front matter (title page, verso, preface, and introduction) or an "About-the-Author" section will provide information on the authors, their credentials, their affiliations, other works, honors, etc. In other words, you can assume that a printed resource from an established publisher, such as Macmillan, is reliable; others have conducted the evaluation for you.

On the other hand, it can be extremely difficult to discover who actually provided the information on an electronic Web site. Locating author information for Web pages frequently involves "going back a layer or two" in the Web site. Some items to look for include who provided the information, why, and explicit statements of authority.

Objectivity

The objectivity and fairness of a source are also important considerations in the evaluation of resources. Objectivity includes coverage of the topics provided (the goals and objectives have to be clearly stated to determine coverage) and the factual, objective, and unbiased nature of the information. Ask yourself if the author or contributor have biases. How reliable are the facts presented? This can be a bit tougher than establishing authority—even for print resources. However, print materials often have a statement of purpose that fundamentally helps to answer these questions. You can usually find this in the preface, introduction, or table of contents. Nonetheless, in many print resources establishing the level of objectivity and bias is more complicated than that.

One effective way to discover if a work is biased is to look at the coverage of controversial issues and the balance of coverage given to various subjects. For example, if you are researching the subject of abortion, ask if the author is pro-choice, pro-life, or unbiased. You might read the material briefly to check about the author (his or her credentials, etc.). See what the chapter titles are like. Remember, however, that biased material can also be a valuable part of your research as long as you balance it with something equally biased in the other direction.

Here are some other tips for ascertaining bias in print materials:

1. Check the illustrations for balance of presentation.
2. Check the content for disparaging comments or slanted perspectives.
3. Look at the lifestyles portrayed; notice if they slant to one culture/people or another.
4. Watch for loaded words, such as "primitive," "savage," "lazy," "evil," "ignorant," etc.
5. Look at the copyright date and consider how attitudes may have changed since the resource was created.

For online sources, consider if a Web site was developed as a means of advertisement or to present scholarly material? The creator of the information may serve as an indicator of biases on electronic sites. For example, was it created by the Disney Corporation? If so, it could be biased towards Disney products and services.

Currency

All resources should be checked for currency, which is fairly straight-forward with print resources. The copyright date is normally (and should be) on the title page or verso. However, consider whether there is a more current edition, or is this the most up-to-date information concerning the topic you are researching. Also check the bibliography and footnotes. Were they current at the time of publication? Although identifying currency in print materials is not problematic, you must also look at other resources (print, nonprint, and Internet) to locate the most up-to-date information for your particular research project. For example, if you are writing a research paper regarding the effects of the Internet on personal communication using statistics from 1994, your information will clearly be out-of-date.

In establishing the currency of relevant information on an electronic site, check document headers and footers. Look for posting and revision dates, policy statements on information maintenance, and link maintenance. It is also significant to recognize that there is no guarantee that a particular page will reside in the same location today as it did yesterday. If you plan to use the information and cite it, a good strategy is to note the date and time you visit the site.

Scope

Scope refers to the basic breadth-and-depth question: What is covered and in what detail? The scope should reflect the purpose of the resource and its intended audience. Has the creator of the information accomplished what was intended? Aspects of scope include subject, geographic location, and time period. Evaluating scope includes reviewing topical aspects of the subject of the resource and noting if there are any key omissions. For example, let's assume you are conducting research on wars from 1950–2000. One resource you consult does not include the Gulf War. What does this say about the scope of this material? Discovering the scope of a resource may take a little time, but it is well worth the effort.

For printed materials, the statement of purpose is generally found in the preface or introduction, and you can use that as a reference point when evaluating scope. For an electronic resource, look for the stated purpose on the site, along with any limitations that may apply and any comments on site's comprehensiveness. Information about nonprint resources, such as CD-ROMs and DVDs, can often be found in the publisher's or vendor's descriptive materials.

Now that you have learned about the fundamentals of evaluating resources, let's find out if this sounds more difficult than it is. You will probably find that it is not necessarily a particularly time-consuming or complex task. Try to evaluate a print resource on your own by doing the exercise "Evaluating a Resource."

You probably know a lot more now than you did before about evaluating print resources, right?

Exercise: Evaluating a Resource

Locate the latest edition of "The Guinness World Book of Records." (Ask any librarian if you don't have a copy.) Look at the information in the front of the book (title and verso pages, preface and introduction) and answer the questions for each section. Following the questions are tips (in italics) to help you answer each question.

1. **Look at the title and verso pages.** *(The title page is usually the first page in a book. It gives information about the creators, publishers, and copyright.)*

Question: Who is the author or creator of this print material?
Tip: *This information should be included either on the title or verso page.*

Question: Can you locate the author or creator's credentials (experience in this area)?
Tip: *This sometimes accompanies the author's name on the title page; other times there may be a section called "about the author" in the front or back of the book. If neither of these methods works, go to www.google.com and type in the author's name in quotation marks.*

Question: What else has the author or creator written on this subject or related topics?
Tip: *Again, this information may be in the front portion of the book. You should also check biographical sources, such as* Biography and Genealogy Master Index, *or you can visit www.google.com, and enter in the author's name. Remember, you can always ask a librarian for assistance.*

Question: What edition is this resource?
Tip: *If the book is not the first edition, look on the cover of the book, the title page, or on the verso page—for example, 2nd ed. or revised edition.*

Question: Who published this resource?
Tip: *The publisher information should be located on the verso of the title page.*

(continued on next page)

Exercise: Evaluating a Resource *(continued)*

Question: Is the publisher reputable?
Tip: *This information may be difficult to locate. Generally, you know if a publisher is reputable because you have heard of them—for example, National Geographic. If you do not recognize the name, you might call a librarian or search the Internet for further information about this publisher.*
2. Now read the preface or introduction of the material.

Question: What is the purpose for writing this resource?
Tip: *The purpose should be stated at the beginning in the preface or introduction.*

Question: Are the goals and objectives clearly stated?
Tip: *The goals and objectives will normally appear in the preface. They should be clear and concise, for example, "This book explains 'Feng Shui,' the Chinese way to harmony." More precise objectives should follow the goal statement.*

Question: Does this source use correct grammar, spelling, and sentence structure?
Tip: *For this, you will need to scan the material. Begin with the preface or introduction and note spelling, grammar, and sentence structure. These are indicators of scholarly—or nonscholarly—materials.*

Question: Who is the audience?
Tip: *Check the preface or introduction. You should find why the material was written, what follows in the text, specialized language or jargon, and other pertinent information. For example, "This textbook is for undergraduate and graduate students studying to be school library media specialists."*

Question: Does the author or creator have a bias(es)? If so, what? How do you know?
Tip: *Answering this can be a bit difficult. First, note the author and publisher. If the publisher is the Pro-Choice Association, this would be a clue. Next, check the preface or introduction, which explains what the resource is all about. If you still can't find this information, scan the resource to see if it includes controversial issues, dated illustrations, slanted perspectives, and loaded words (such as "primitive" or "savage"). Also note the copyright date.*

Question: Does the resource provide balanced representations of cultural, ethnic, and racial groups? How can you tell?

(continued on next page)

Exercise: Evaluating a Resource *(continued)*

Tip: *Again, this may not be immediately apparent. It is part of determining bias, so take another look at author, publisher, preface, table of contents, and illustrations. Any or all of these may assist you in assessing balance.*

Question: How did the author or creator obtain the data? Is this possible to determine?
Tip: *If this information is available, it should be included in the preface or introduction. Otherwise, attempt to contact the creator to determine how the data was obtained.*

Question: Are the contents based on personal opinion, research, interviews, case studies?
Tip: *Again, if this information is available, it should be in the preface or introduction. For instance, it might state, "The information in this book is based on the culmination of research studies conducted by X and Y.*

3. Look at the table of contents.

Question: Are there significant attachments or appendixes? If so, what are they? Are they useful or necessary?
Tip: *The table of contents can tell you a great deal about the resource. First, it should be easy to follow. There should be a sufficient number of subheadings to provide a broad outline. Look at the appendixes or attachments. Do they relate to the content or are they merely "add-ons." Do they provide additional, useful information?*

Question: Does the resource contain a table of contents, preface, introduction, glossary, or index?
Tip: *This is easy; merely scan the book. A table of contents is a must to guide you through the material. The preface or introduction is particularly useful in that it explains why the resource was written and what it is about. Glossaries are helpful for sources with unfamiliar or technical terms. An index can assist you in locating particular information quickly.*

4. Read through some of the book.

Question: Is the information clear, comprehensive, and easy to read?
Tip: *Scan the resource. It should be easy to follow, with appropriate headings and subheadings. The words should not be too technical for you and it should be long enough and broad enough to cover the subject or topic.*

Question: If visuals are used, are they useful and unambiguous?

(continued on next page)

Exercise: Evaluating a Resource (*continued*)

Tip: *Illustrations can be very helpful—or they can be purely aesthetic. Visuals should complement the text, explaining it more thoroughly or more clearly.*

5. How does it compare with other materials?

Question: Is the information still accurate? How do you know? (Have you viewed other materials?)
Tip: *This requires more work, including looking at additional resources. Many things—for example technology, geography, medicine—change so rapidly that in addition to checking the copyright date, you should compare it with other sources. Often Internet sources are helpful, as they tend to be current—but be certain that they are accurate, as well.*

Question: Was the print resource reviewed? Where does the review appear? Is it positive or negative?
Tip: *This may take a little looking. Ask your librarian for assistance with locating review sources. Reviews may be found online, for example, on amazon.com. Remember, however, that review sources vary from informal to scholarly—for example, a review in* New York Times Book Review *would probably be more valid than one by a reader on amazon.com.*

EVALUATING NONPRINT INFORMATION AND THE INTERNET

Hope Tillman (2001), Director of Libraries at Babson College, explains that the growth of information on the Internet and the development of more sophisticated searching tools, has made it more likely that one can find information and answers to real questions. However, within the chaos of networked data are not only valuable pieces of information but also an incredible amount of rubbish.

When evaluating nonprint materials, such as videotapes, CD-ROMs, and DVDs, the same four evaluation criteria apply. It is worth the effort because these formats are available in libraries and for purchase and present useful information in a different way. You will need to alter criteria slightly to fit the specific format. Let's look at an example (see the Exercise on the next page). First, look at the criteria (accuracy/authority, objectivity, currency, and scope), and read the following questions while thinking about how nonprint formats differ from print formats. Following the questions are tips for answering these questions.

As you can see, evaluating nonprint materials includes many of the same criteria and questions as evaluating print materials. However, the nature of the format requires the application of additional criteria.

Exercise: Evaluating a Videodisc

A videodisc is similar to an audio CD, but it is larger and contains still images and movies in addition to sound and music—also called a laserdisc: The evaluation for a videodisc can be used for any nonprint resource.

1. Look at the cover and accompanying ancillary materials.

Question: Is the creator an expert on this subject? How do you know?
Tip: *Just as for a print resource, reliabile creators are usually known. If you do not know the creator, ask other people (particularly your librarian) or attempt to locate information about the person on the Internet—for instance, via google.com.*

Question: Who published the videodisc? Are they reputable? Have they produced others?
Tip: *The same approach applies for the publisher's reputation as for the creators. Do some digging around to see what you can find out.*

Question: Are specific instructions included? Are they easy to understand?
Tip: *Many nonprint resources include useful—or even necessary—instructions for using the materials. Like all instructions, they should be in an easy-to-understand-and-use format—always look over the instructions first.*

Question: Is technical support readily available?
Tip: *Not all nonprint resources will require technical support, but if the format does involve technical support, it should be easily accessible at any time of the day or night. Of course, live and 24/7 is preferable.*

Question: Are ancillary materials (such as worksheets and activity pages) included? Do you find them helpful?
Tip: *Many nonprint materials include worksheets and activities that make the format much more useful. These materials should be complementary to the information, not simply decorative.*

(continued on next page)

Exercise: Evaluating a Videodisc (*continued*)

Question: Can you locate reviews of this videodisc? Are they positive or negative?
Tip: *Again, reviews of nonprint materials can be found in a variety of review sources and online. Ask your librarian for a list of these sources.*

2. View the videodisc.

Question: Is the videodisc free of content errors?
Tip: *Just as with print materials, nonprint resources should present correct and authoritative information. Scan the resource prior to viewing it in-depth.*

Question: Does it include current information? Is there another source that is more current?
Tip: *Again, as with print sources, the information should be current. However, the copyright date is not always a good indication. View the resource, checking for up-to-date information. Enjoying the format is not enough; you need to use it for correct, objective, and current information.*

Question: Is the videodisc appropriate for your intended purpose?
Tip: *Although a videodisc may be titled "Recycling," it may only touch on one or two aspects of recycling and not be sufficient for your needs. Scan it before borrowing or purchasing it.*

Question: Is the information of sufficient scope to adequately cover your topic?
Tip: *As with print materials, the information should have enough "breadth and depth" to cover the topic you are researching.*

Question: Are the concepts and vocabulary relevant?
Tip: *At times it may be difficult to know if nonprint material is appropriate for you. The "Recycling" videodisc, for example, may be appropriate for elementary school children only.*

Question: Is the videodisc "user friendly?"
Tip: *All nonprint materials should be easy to use, and instructions easy to follow. For example, be certain that it is easy to move from place to place when using a videodisc.*

Question: Is the videodisc objective and does it include a balanced presentation of the topic?
Tip: *By viewing the source, you should be able to determine objectivity and bias. Listen to what is said as well as viewing the images—both can be clues.*

(continued on next page)

Exercise: Evaluating a Videodisc (continued)
Question: Does the videodisc provide a balanced representation of cultural, ethnic, and racial groups? **Tip:** *As with objectivity and bias, you can identify a balanced representation by viewing and listening to the videodisc and reading accompanying ancillary information.* **Question:** Does it include appropriate, high-quality visuals? Is the sound clear? **Tip:** *Just as with a print resource, the visuals should be understandable and contain information pertinent to the topic. Likewise, the sound must be clear and understandable.*

COMPARING NONPRINT TO PRINT

To conduct accurate research, it is necessary to examine a wide variety of sources and formats and compare them with each other. Suppose you want to research global warming. It is a good idea to evaluate the information on a Web site with the information in printed periodicals and published books. A Web site on global warming may include videos, photographs, audio, a tutorial—all useful in understanding this concept. Likewise, the periodical may have been written by a scholar in the field and include exceptionally current information on one or more aspects of global warming. A book on the topic might be quite comprehensive and include a history of the subject; however, it may not address the most recent information on the topic.

INTERNET EVALUATION

There are a few fundamental considerations involved with Internet research. Unlike printed sources and even other multimedia sources that must be screened, anyone with the right software and access to the Internet can publish a document on the Web, regardless of accuracy or quality of presentation. Another matter for concern is that the creator, at any time and as often as desired, can alter Web pages. What is here today may be gone tomorrow. There are four types of Web sites; these are shown in the box, "Exploring Types of Web Sites," on the next page.

Remember, no matter what resource you are using, ask yourself why you are using it. Is it because it is handy? Easy to read? On the Web?

Short? You should search for resources that are appropriate for the information you are seeking. All types of materials can be good. Likewise, all resources have the potential of being useless. Evaluate what you read; learn to discern and discriminate information—all of it—*learn to learn!* It is up to you to sift through the seemingly endless array of materials and locate those few sources that are ideal for your research. Research is not an easy task. It can, however, be an enlightening undertaking. Once you learn to locate, use, and evaluate information, you are on your way to becoming an information literate person—one who knows how to be a lifelong learner.

Exploring Types of Web Sites

1. *Informational Pages*, such as scholarly research and fact sheets. Many government sites are Informational Pages.

American FactFinder

> *http://factfinder.census.gov/servlet/BasicFactsServlet*

This page is an example of a government Web site (from the U.S. Census Bureau), an informational page.

2. *News and Journalistic Sources*, such as online periodicals, magazines, and newspapers.

WHAS11

> *www.whas11.com*

This is a news and journalistic source.

3. *Advocacy Pages*, such as Web sites that take a particular view of an issue. Many of these sites end with ".com" or ".org."

4. *Personal Home Pages*, which are informal and vary widely.

Dr. Barbara Foster's Homepage

> *http://www.spalding.edu/faculty/frame.asp*

This is an example of a personal home page.

Exercise: Viewing Web Sites I

Let's look at the evaluation criteria (accuracy/authority, objectivity, currency, and scope)—this time with regard to the Internet. While viewing the Web site "Beef Nutrition," answer the following questions. For each question there is a tip to help you:

1. **Explore the Web site *http://beefnutrition.org* and answer the following questions (refer to the tips in italics):**

Question: Who is the author or creator of the site? Can you contact this person(s)?
Tip: *On any Web site, at the very least, the creator's name should appear along with an e-mail address. Typically, this information is found at the bottom portion of the home page.*

Question: Is the author or creator of the Web site qualified to write this work? How do you know? Does the author have any other publications?
Tip: *Of course, this varies with the type of Web site—informational, personal, etc. However, Beef Nutrition should state not only who created it, but also the creator's credentials. Research the author/creator. Go to the Web site www.google.com to see if the person has created other sites or is affiliated with a reputable organization. Remember to put quotation marks around the person's name.*

Question: What are the purpose, goals, and objectives of this Web site?
Tip: *It should be easy to locate the purpose, goals, and objectives of a Web site. Beef Nutrition should explain why it is written, for whom it is written, and what you will learn by visiting the Web site. Look at the entire site, including all links.*

Question: Why was this site produced?
Tip: *This should be obvious from the site itself. First, check the domain (.com, .org, etc.), which may give some clues. For example, a .gov (government) site is produced for people interested in various aspects of the United States government or interested in information published by the government. Next, examine the Web site to determine its purpose. Is it for information, advertising, or aesthetics?*

(continued on next page)

Exercise: Viewing Web Sites I *(continued)*

Question: Who published the site? Are the publisher's qualifications on the site?

Tip: *Publisher information, like creator information, should be available on the home page, typically at the bottom of the home page. It does make a difference. If Beef Nutrition were published by the Poultry Association of America it would be important to know that.*

Question: How detailed is the information?

Tip: *Look at the entire Web site, including all links. Many sites are sources of more information than is at first apparent because they guide you to additional information via links.*

Question: Does the author or creator express opinions? If so, are they clearly labeled?

Tip: *If the creator of the Web site takes a particular stance, it should be explained within the site.*

Question: Does this site include advertising? (Is this necessarily bad?)

Tip: *Not all advertising Web sites are bad. Actually, many include quite useful information. Be careful, however; remain aware that the creator is advertising something and look at all sides of the story.*

Question: When was the Web site created? Is it obvious? When was it last updated?

Tip: *The date that the Web site was created, along with the date it was last updated, should be clearly displayed on the home page, usually on the bottom portion.*

Question: What does this site offer that you cannot find elsewhere?

Tip: *Ideally, this format will offer new or different information, or at least a unique approach. The format allows video, photographs, visuals, and audio. View the entire Web site to ascertain why this information is particularly useful for your research.*

Question: How current are the links? Are they useful? Are they easy to navigate?

Tip: *Although the Web site itself may be current—and newly updated—that does not mean that the links are current. Check out all links and see when they were last updated. At times, creators of Web sites regularly update the site itself, but do not take the time to ensure that the links are current—or even still exist.*

(continued on next page)

Exercise: Viewing Web Sites 1 *(continued)*

Question: Is there a balance between images and text?

Tip: *Visuals and text should complement each other to explain information more thoroughly. Although a particular Web site will logically include either more visuals or more text, view the sites for balance and specified purpose.*

Question: Is the site free of grammatical errors?

Tip: *As with a print or other nonprint resources, Web sites should be grammatically correct and free of spelling errors. Blatant grammatical errors should tell you something about the accuracy and authority of the Web site.*

Exercise: Viewing Web Sites 2

Web sites differ greatly! They differ in quality, size, number of links, accuracy, currency, to name a few ways. Examine the following Web sites on the *evaluation* of Web-based sources. Note the differences in the Web sites. Some are very interactive, some include videos and illustrations, some provide useful links, some are amateur, and some are professional. By looking at these sites, you can better determine what type of information is available on the Internet. After visiting them, consider the following:

1. Are the sites informational, journalistic, advocacy pages, or personal home pages? How do you know?
2. Can the authors or creators be clearly identified? If so, who are they?
3. Are the purposes of the Web site easy to identify? What are they?
4. Why do you think the sites were produced? How can you tell?
5. Can you determine who published the sites? Who?
6. Is the information on the sites you are linked to current? How do you know?
7. Are there any spelling or grammatical errors on the sites?

Why is it important to know all of this about Web sites? After all, it *is* in "black-and-white"—that means it is *fact*, right?

The Good, the Bad and the Ugly

http://lib.nmsu.edu/staff/susabeck/evalcrit.html

(continued on next page)

Exercise: Viewing Web Sites 2 (continued)

This site discusses why it is a good idea to evaluate Web sources. It includes examples, criteria, suggestions, and a bibliography.

QUICK: The Quality Information Checklist

www.quick.org.uk/menu.htm

This site includes eight ways of checking information on Web sites.

Criteria for Evaluation of Internet Information Resources

www.vuw.ac.nz/~agsmith/evaln

This site discusses criteria for evaluation of Internet information resources.

Critically Analyzing Information Sources

www.library.cornell.edu/okuref/research/skill26.htm

This Web site, from the Cornell University Library, discusses analyzing information sources.

Information Literacy: The Web Is Not an Encyclopedia

www.inform.umd.edu/LibInfo/literacy

This site is from the University of Maryland.

Evaluating Web Resources

www2.widener.edu/Wolfgram-Memorial-Library/webevaluation/webeval.htm

This Web site, by Marsha Ann Tate and Jan Alexander, is an organized, useful site with numerous links.

Evaluating Internet "Research"

www.vmi.edu/library/kw/evaluate.htm

This Web site examines the evaluation of Internet research.

CONCLUSION

When in doubt, doubt. You are fortunate to have enormous amounts of information readily available. Or are you? Because of the information explosion of the twenty-first century, it is now necessary to critically evaluate all that you read. No longer can one say that if it is in "black-and-white" is it fact.

This chapter has provided basic information regarding evaluation of print, nonprint, and Internet resources. Research in the twenty-first century requires active evaluation of materials. You must become an information literate individual—one who knows how to find, use, and evaluate the information you need. In today's world, knowing these things will be your ticket to endless learning.

REFERENCES AND FURTHER READING

Anderson, Mary Alice. 2001. "So Much Information." *Multimedia Schools,* 8: 22–24.

Auer, Nicole. 1998. "Bibliography on Evaluating Internet Resources." *Emergency Librarian,* 25: 23–24.

Brandt, D. Scott. 1996. "Evaluating Information on the Internet." *Computers in Libraries,* 16: 44–47.

Collins, Boyd. 1996. "Web Watch." *Library Journal,* 32.

Connell, H. Tschera, and Jennifer E. Tipple. 1999. "Testing the Accuracy of Information on the World Wide Web Using the AltaVista Search Engine." *Reference & User Services Quarterly,* 360–368.

Cottrell. Janet R. 2001. "Teaching Students to Evaluate Web Sources More Critically: Implications from a Faculty Workshop." *College & Research Libraries News,* 62: 141–143.

Cunningham, Sally Jo. 1997. "Teaching Students to Critically Evaluate the Quality of Internet Research Resources." *SIGCSE Bulletin,* 31–34.

Fitzgerald, Mary Ann. 1997. "Misinformation on the Internet: Applying Evaluation Skills to Online Information." *Emergency Librarian,* 24: 9–14.

Fox, Lynne M. 1996. "Some On-line (and Off-line) Resources for Evaluating Information on the World Wide Web." *Colorado Libraries,* 46–47.

Gardner, Susan A., Hiltraut H. Benham, and Bridget M. Newell. 1999. "Oh, What a Tangled Web We've Woven! Helping Students Evaluate Sources." *English Journal,* 89: 39–44.

Hahn, Susan E. 1997. "Internet: Let the User Beware." *Reference Services Review,* 25: 7–13.

Jacobson, Trudi, and Laura Cohen. 1997. "Teaching Students to Evaluate Internet Sites." *The Teaching Professor,* 11: 4.

Kapoun, Jim. 1998. "Teaching Undergrads WEB Evaluation." *College and Research Libraries News,* 59: 522–523.

Lederer, Naomi. 2000. "New Form(at): Using the Web to Teach Research and Critical Thinking Skills." *Reference Services Review,* 28: 130–153.

McBride, Kari Boyd, and Ruth Dickstein. 1998. "The Web Demands Critical Reading by Students." *Chronicle of Higher Education,* 44: B6.

McKenzie, Jamie. 1996. "Making WEB Meaning." *Educational Leadership,* 54: 30–32.

Makulowich, John. 1996. "Quality Control on the Net." *Database,* 93–94.

Nowicki, Stacy, 1999. Information Literacy and Critical Thinking in the Electronic Environment. *Journal of Instruction Delivery Systems,* 13: 25–28.

O'Grady, Alice, 1999. "Information Literacy Skills and the Senior Project." *Educational Leadership,* 57: 61–62.

Pagell, Ruth A. 1995. "Quality and the Internet: An Open Letter." *Online,* 7–9.

Rothenberg, David, 1997. "How the Web Destroys the Quality of Students' Research Papers." *Chronicle of Higher Education*: A44.

Sabol, Laurie, 1998. "The Value of Student Evaluation of a Web Site." *Research Strategies,* 16: 79–84.

Safford, Barbara Ripp. 1996. "The Problem with the Internet: It is NOT the Information Highway." *School Library Media Activities Monthly* 13: 42–43.

Safford, Barbara Ripp, and others. 1996. "What Do We Teach about the World Wide Web?" *School Library Media Activities Monthly,* 13: 44–46.

Schrock, Kathleen. 1996. "It Must Be True. I Found It on the Internet." *Technology Connection,* 3: 12–14.

Sciba, Ann, 2001. "Practice Makes Perfect (or at Least We Hope So)." *Book Report,* 20: 26–29.

Skov, Annette, 1998. "Separating the Wheat from the Chaff: Internet Quality." *Database*: 38–40.

Smith, Alastair G. 1997. "Testing the Surf: Criteria for Evaluating Internet Information Resources." *The Public-Access Computer Systems Review*: 8.

Tate, Marsha, and Jane Alexander. 1996. "Teaching Critical Evaluation Skills for World Wide Web Resources." *Computers in Libraries,* 16: 49–54.

Tillman, Hope N. 2001. "Evaluating Quality on the Net." Retrieved February 24, 2001 from *www.hopetillman.com/findqual.html*

Vine, Rita. 2001. "Real People Don't Do Boolean: How to Teach End Users to Find High-Quality Information on the Internet." *Information Outlook,* 5: 16–23.

Chapter 7

What Are Copyright and Plagiarism All About?

Let's begin with simple definitions. *Copyright* is a legal protection that provides the creator of a work with the sole right to publish, reproduce, and sell that work. To clarify this definition, look at it personally. You just spent the entire summer writing a terrific play. You put the play on your home page. Later, you discover that someone else has produced and claimed credit for your play. That is copyright infringement—makes you angry, right? You deserve credit (and income) for your creation. Anyone who creates something in a permanent form (e.g., written, recorded, painted) is the owner of that creation and is protected by copyright law. In other words, an idea in your head is not protected by copyright, but if you write it, record it, paint it, or otherwise put that idea into a permanently recorded format, it is now copyright protected; it belongs to you.

Plagiarism is turning in someone else's work as your own (remember the play you produced?). In other words, plagiarism is dishonest—and illegal. Everyone deserves and has the right to credit for an original creation. Academic (dis)honesty is an age-old problem. However, with the arrival of the Internet, plagiarizing is easier than ever before. This does not mean that you cannot use a portion of someone else's work. It is perfectly acceptable to "borrow" someone's idea, if—and only if—you give him or her proper credit.

COPYRIGHT AND PRINT RESOURCES

Public Domain

First, it is important to understand some basic points regarding copyright. If a work is in the *public domain,* you may use it without

79

permission. What is the public domain? It comprises all works that are not copyright-protected. These works may be borrowed without permission. Examples of works in the public domain are materials produced by the United States government, or older works for which copyright has expired.

Public Domain

For further information, visit the following Web sites:

Music Works Public Domain

> *http://pubdomain.com*

This site is an authoritative resource for locating outstanding works of music in the United States Public Domain.

Copyright Web Site: Public Domain

> *www.benedict.com/info/publicDomain/publicDomain.asp*

This Web site discusses a variety of topics regarding public domain, such as lost copyright, expired copyright, government documents, and works granted to the public domain.

How to Determine When a Work is in Public Domain

> *http://quotations.about.com/c/ht/00/07/How_Determine_Work_*
> *Public0962933548.htm*

This Web site addresses how to determine when a work is in public domain.

Fair Use

Fair use is a more complicated concept than public domain. Carol Simpson, a library science professor at the University of North Texas and an expert in copyright issues for schools, explains, "Fair use provisions of the copyright law grant particular types of users conditional rights to use or reproduce certain copyrighted materials as long as the reproduction or use of those materials meets defined guidelines" (Simpson, 2001: 13). These guidelines are quite lengthy and specific. Remember that fair use guidelines are exactly that—guidelines, not laws. They are merely interpretations of exceptions to copyright law agreed upon by a large number of institutions and organizations.

    As Simpson stated:

Ever since the first copyright statute was enacted, the primary focus of the law has been to protect the authors and publishers of books and other print media. Until the invention of the printing press, no one worried much about illegal copying or distribution that might injure a copyright holder. Copying was so tedious and labor-intensive there were few legal copies and fewer illegal ones. Cheap and easy mass printing made theft or misappropriation of an author's works much easier. In today's world, modern technology has made reproduction and distribution of almost any work or image nearly instantaneous (2001: 21).

You might think that obtaining copyright is a difficult task. This is not the case. Under United States copyright law, anything original and creative put in a tangible form is protected by copyright—and the protection is automatic, from the moment you create something. Remember: This includes e-mail and Web pages! So, why would you bother to register a copyright application? There are three primary reasons to do so:

1. You have your copyrighted material on the public record and receive a certificate of registration.
2. You have the ability to sue.
3. Your copyright registration will assist you with statutory damages and attorney's fees.

Fair Use

Copyright Web Site: Fair Use

www.copyrightwebsite.com/info/fairUse/fairUse.asp

This Web site addresses the fair use provision of the copyright act—the statutory decree.

Copyright Law and Fair Use

www-sul.stanford.edu/cpyright.html

This site serves as a guide that addresses issues concerning the use of copyrighted material in an academic setting.

Fair Use Guidelines for Educational Multimedia

www.indiana.edu/~ccumc/mmfairuse.html

This Web site discusses fair use guidelines for educational multimedia.

Registering Copyright

For additional information concerning this issue, visit the following Web sites:

Why Register a Copyright Application?

www.copyrightwebsite.com/info/registration/why.asp

This Web site discusses the reasons to register and the dangers of non-registration.

How Do You File a Copyright Application?

www.copyrightwebsite.com/info/registration/how.asp

This site explains how you register a work with the copyright office.

Let's take a look at some other questions you might be asking at this point concerning copyright issues:

Question: What works can I register for copyright protection?
Answer: *Overall, almost any original expression that is fixed in a concrete form. Examples include literary works, musical works, dramatic works, pictorial and graphic works, audiovisual works, sound recordings, architectural works, computer software, and choreography.*

Question: What is not eligible for copyright protection?
Answer: *Not many items, but the following are a few examples: facts, ideas, names, lettering, slogans, procedures, methods, concepts, short phrases, and titles.*

Question: When does copyright protection begin? When does it end?
Answer: *It begins when a work is actually created and fixed in a tangible form. Copyright protection ends after the life of the author plus 70 years. If it was published before 1923, it is not protected unless the copyright has been renewed.*

Question: What about the infamous copyright symbol?
Answer: *The symbol © is also known as copyright notice (an identifier placed on copies of a work to inform the world of copyright ownership). Today, this symbol is optional. Should you wish to use one, however, you have every right to do so, as long as you are the true author of the work.*

Question: How can one "lose" copyright?
Answer: *Essentially copyright is never lost. However, you may "give it away" (a personal choice).*

Question: Is copyright infringement really a crime?
Answer: *Yes. Although copyright law is primarily civil law, copyright violation can be a criminal act and essentially may result a possible felony conviction.*

Exercise: Crash Course in Copyright and Fair Use

Let's take a crash course in copyright. Just follow the tutorial to learn more about issues regarding copyright.

Crash Course in Copyright

www.utsystem.edu/OGC/IntellectualProperty/cprtindx.htm

Now try your skills with this Copyright Tutorial, which covers ownership, fair use, and permission.

Copyright Tutorial

www.lib.utsystem.edu/copyright.

Why look at these Web sites? What's the purpose? Because both of these sites provide interesting and beneficial information about copyright, fair use, etc. It is very important for you to know about this—really. Copyright infringement and plagiarism are *crimes*. Let's look at some questions. See if you can answer them now after taking the tutorials:

- How do you know who owns what? How do you find out?

- How (exactly) do you get permission to use someone else's material?
- What is copyright management? How does it involve *you*?

Do you want a "Crash Course Certificate"? If so, you must explore these sites and answer the 12 test questions correctly!

(continued on next page)

Exercise: Copyright Laws

Copyright Office of the Library of Congress

www.loc.gov/copyright/

This Web site provides information and links regarding law, registration, Library of Congress, Internet Resources, and other pertinent information.

Please visit this Web site and view all links. Answer the following questions based on the information found on the Web site:

- Can a minor claim copyright?
- Does copyright protect architecture?
- How much does it cost to obtain a copyright?
- Can you get a new certificate if you lose yours?
- Can foreigners register their works in the United States?
- Does the Copyright Office have a list of songs and movies in the public domain?
- Can you copyright the name of a band?

List three things that you learned by exploring this Web site:

1. _____

2. _____

3. _____

COPYRIGHT AND NONPRINT RESOURCES

According to Simpson, "Guidelines for use of audiovisual [nonprint] works vary widely. Depending on the medium and the method of acquisition, rights may vary from unlimited to short-lived. The Copyright Act of 1976...clarified many ambiguities..." (2001: 39). However, for all basic purposes, the differences in copyright law (between print and nonprint) are primarily technical and are outweighed by the similarities in the law's application.

I hope that by taking another personal look, this will become clearer for you. Suppose, you are quite an artist and have created a wonderful poster. You scanned this poster and, again, placed it on your home page. Do you have copyright ownership? Yes, you have all five rights of a copyright holder. You may

1. reproduce,
2. distribute,
3. publicly perform,
4. publicly display, and
5. modify the work.

As the creator of this poster, you can decide exactly how you wish it to be used. Now, what is the difference between "cannot" and "not supposed to"? Someone can print out a copy of the poster and send it to friends or display it. Is he or she supposed to? No. Why not? Because the right to do these things is reserved for the copyright holder (in this case, you).

COPYRIGHT AND INTERNET RESOURCES

Internet materials are copyrighted just as print and nonprint materials are, and notification of copyright status is not required.

> Every person who writes a document published on the Internet, who creates a graphic or icon, who scans his own photograph or records his own voice into a digital file, who sends an electronic mail message, who creates a document for a newsgroup, or who designs a Web page owns the copyright to his or her creative work (Simpson, 2001: 111).

Look at it this way: If you see an item you would like to use on your Web page, you must ask permission to use it if it is copyrighted. Therefore, if you want to use a Disney character on your Web page, you would have to contact the Disney Corporation in order to obtain a license to use the image. That license would tell you how you could use the Disney character, how much you would have to pay, and other restrictions and conditions. On the other hand, your original graphics, text, audio, etc., are eligible for copyright protection as soon as you place them on your Web page.

For further information regarding this issue, visit the following Web site:

Franklin Pierce Law Center
www.fplc.edu

This Web site discusses copyright information for Internet authors and artists.

PLAGIARISM

Plagiarism is not a new phenomenon. "Borrowing without permission" has been going on as long as there have been dishonest people (in this case, academics). However, with the advent of the Internet, which provides easy access to immeasurable amounts of research materials, plagiarism has grown enormously. According to Atkins and Nelson (2002), noted authors regarding plagiarism, today millions of "computer savvy" people find it easy to plagiarize. They use someone else's intellectual property as their own without citations or credits. Often students cheat because they think everyone else does. Students are capable of changing their ways if colleges clearly demand honesty, engage students in addressing ethical issues, and put them in charge of enforcement.

Why do people plagiarize? A few reasons include:

- a lack of knowledge regarding plagiarism,
- a lack of knowledge regarding information on the Internet,
- a lack of confidence in one's ability to write a paper,
- a lack of knowledge regarding citing sources, and
- procrastination.

Do any of these ring a bell?
Plagiarism is not merely copying someone else's work word-for-word. Actually, plagiarism comes in four basic forms:

1. *Exact*: Copying a source word-for-word with no credit given to the creator.
2. *Borrowing*: Turning in a paper that someone else has written (a major problem with the arrival of "paper mills" on the Internet).
3. *Unclear*: Lack of indicating where the borrowing begins and ends.
4. *Medley*: Copying of a resource using a few words here and there and not providing credit to the creator.

As you can easily see, plagiarism is a relatively simple feat—but dishonest and illegal. So, how do you keep from plagiarizing? The following are useful tips:

- Be aware of what plagiarism entails (it's a *crime*).
- Allow yourself time to write the paper—do not procrastinate.
- Make certain that all research assignments are absolutely clear.
- Sharpen your time management and planning skills.
- Learn effective research and writing skills.
- Use a variety of resources for your research (for example, Internet resources, print resources, personal interviews, etc.).
- Take notes when conducting research, writing down the full source of information.
- Conduct research using critical-thinking and problem-solving skills—moving away from the "cut and paste" mode of research.
- Write drafts and make copies of research materials.
- Cite your sources—if you are unsure, cite them anyway!
- Include an annotated bibliography (discussed in Chapter 8) with your research paper.
- Use current references (within the last two years) if your topic requires recent information.
- Include bibliography cards, note cards, photocopies of sources, and outlines with your final paper.
- Be confident in what you write—research it, study it, and reflect on it.
- Do not succumb to pressures from peers or others.
- Take pride in your work.
- Get help if you are confused or uncertain.
- Remember that you would not want someone else to "borrow" your work without giving you proper credit.

It is also helpful to learn how to perform the following and to know the difference:

1. *Paraphrase:* Restate the information in your own words. This does not require that you use quotation marks, but it does require proper citation.
2. *Summarize:* This is similar to a paraphrase, but it is shorter and even closer to your own words. Proper citation (no quotation marks) is required.
3. *Quote:* You may copy word-for-word, but this requires quotation marks and proper citation.

Detecting Plagiarism

The Instructors Guide to Internet Plagiarism

www.plagiarized.com

This Web site offers suggestions of what to look for if plagiarism is suspected.

Solutions for a New Era in Education

http://turnitin.com

This Web site scans student papers to detect plagiarism.

Internet Plagiarism

www.plagiarism.org

This Web site attempts to stop online plagiarism by verifying student work against Web sites using mathematical functions.

Internet Paper Mills

www.coastal.edu/library/mills2.htm

This Web site provides a listing of numerous paper-mill sites.

Two general Web sites concerning plagiarism information:

Virtual Salt: Anti-Plagiarism Strategies for Research Papers

www.virtualsalt.com/antiplag.htm

This Web site addresses anti-plagiarism strategies for research papers.

Copyright: Libraries and the Public

www.ala.org/oitp/copyright

This site, the American Library Association's Office for Information Technology Policy (OTIP) Web site, includes an interview with a copyright specialist.

The Center for Academic Integrity

www.academicintegrity.org/cai_research.asp

This Web site discusses six major research projects that have had disturbing, provocative, and challenging results.

Internet Paper Mills

What is a *paper mill,* anyway? Actually, these monsters existed long before the Internet. However, with the advent of the Internet, the number of locations where paper mills are available has grown infinitely, and the ease with which papers can be obtained has increased immensely. Paper mills allow you to directly purchase or download pre-written research papers. This is dishonest and illegal.

Internet paper-mill Web sites provide papers at no cost or for a fee. You should be aware, however, that instructors are now better equipped to detect use of these sites. The following are examples of Internet sites that assist in detecting paper mill plagiarism.

Internet Paper Mills
Cyberessays.com
www.cyberessays.com
This site offers free term papers, essays and reports.
Academictermpapers.com
www.academictermpapers.com
Through this site, you can order custom-made papers at the cost of $7.00 a page.

CONCLUSION

Copyright and plagiarism are not new, but they are new issues for many people. They are as much ethical as legal issues. It may take time to develop a strong, foolproof method to address and, eventually, prevent infringement of copyright and plagiarism. Instructors should inform you, and other students, about plagiarism and copyright and address these issues in a variety of ways. It is critical that you become aware of the seriousness of these problems. Students like you, who use critical thinking and original thoughts, are less likely to infringe on copyright or plagiarize. Today's global, technological society provides many challenges; not all of them positive. It is up to you to remain honest—to make the first priority to *learn to learn*.

REFERENCES AND FURTHER READING

Anderson, Judy, 1998. *Stop, Thief!* Jefferson, NC: McFarland.

Anderson, Judy. 2001. "Give Print a Chance." *School Library Journal*, 37.

Atkins, T., and G. Nelson. 2001. "Plagiarism and the Internet: Turning the Tables." *English Journal*, 90: 101–104.

Colon, Aly. 2001. "Avoid the Pitfalls of Plagiarism." *Writer*, 114: 8.

Dukelow, Ruth H. 1992. *The Library Copyright Guide*. Washington, DC: Copyright Information Services, Association for Educational Communications and Technology.

Hickman, John. 1998. "Cybercheats: Term Paper Shopping Online." *New Republic*, 218: 14.

Hoffman, Gretchen McCord. 2001. *Copyright in Cyberspace: Questions and Answers for Librarians*. New York: Neal-Schuman.

Laird, E. 2001. "We All Pay for Internet Plagiarism." *Education Digest*, 67: 56–59.

Lathrop, Ann, and Kathleen Foss. 2000. *Student Cheating and Plagiarism in the Internet Era: A Wake-Up Call*. Greenwood Village, CO: Libraries Unlimited.

Lincoln, Margaret. 2002. "Internet Plagiarism." *Multimedia Schools*, 9.

Logan, Debra. 2000. "Imitation on the Web: Flattery, Fair Use, or Felony?" *Knowledge Quest*, 28: 16–18.

McCabe, Donald. May 2001. "Students' Plagiarism from Net Is Normal." *Houston Chronicle*, 5.

McCarroll, Christina. 28 August 2001. "Beating Web Cheaters at Their Own Game." *Christian Science Monitor*, 16.

Miller, Pamela C. 1979. "Copyright: When Is Fair Use Not Fair:?" *Educational Technology*, 19: 44–47.

Ralston, Neil. 2001. "Copyright in the Classroom." *Quill*, 89: 28.

Renard, L. 2000. "Cut and Paste 101: Plagiarism and the Net." *Educational Leadership*, 38–42.

Schemo, Diana Jean. 2001. "University of Virginia Hit by Scandal over Cheating." *New York Times*, May 10.

Simpson, Carol. 2001. *Copyright for Schools: A Practical Guide*. (3rd ed.). Worthington, OH: Linworth.

Software and Information Industry Association. Education Software Management. 1994. *A K–12 Guide to Legal Software Use*. The Author.

Stim, Richard. 2000. *Getting Permission: How to License and Clear Copyrighted Materials Online and Off*. Berkeley, CA: Nolo Press.

Weiss, Kenneth. 13 February 2000. *Focus on Ethics Can Curb Cheating, Colleges Find*. The Los Angeles Times.

Chapter 8

How Do I Give Credit to the Creator of the Information I Read?

This chapter discusses how to *cite* resources, that is, give credit to the information sources you will use to write your research paper or develop your presentation. Academic disciplines use certain conventions, called styles, for citing sources. This chapter introduces three commonly used styles.

- *Chicago Manual of Style,*
- *Modern Language Association Handbook for Writers of Research Papers* (MLA), and
- *Publication Manual of the American Psychological Association Style* (APA).

It is vital that you provide proper credit to the people who created the information. Thus, correct citing of information used is an essential aspect of research.

CITATION STYLES AND SOURCES

Although there are numerous citation styles, three of the most commonly used styles are the *Chicago Manual of Style*, the Modern Language Association (MLA), and the American Psychological Association (APA). All of these have printed manuals that explain the style in detail and how to use it when writing a research paper. All three styles have some basic parts in common, but the organization is somewhat different. The styles prescribe how to cite the references within the text itself (parenthetical references) and also how to cite them at the end of the research paper (bibliography page or reference list):

- *Parenthetical references* are used to cite your sources within the paper itself. See Figure 8.1 on the next page for an example of how parenthetical references appear in a research paper.

93

Research and Problem-Solving Processes and Models

Our complex global society continues to expand at a rate beyond our capacity to comprehend. Access to, comprehension, evaluation, and use of information are needed to ease the burden of change and assist humanity in navigating its course towards the future. It is imperative that students possess the skills to learn efficiently and effectively. Explicitly discussing research and problem-solving strategies makes it more likely that students will transfer these processes to future research and problem-solving situations.

The following three processes or models are widely accepted and used as problem-solving strategies in schools today: *Information Seeking* by Carol Kuhlthau, the *Big6™ Information Problem-Solving Model* by Michael Eisenberg and Robert Berkowitz, and the *Research Process* by Barbara Stripling and Judy Pitts. (Figure 1.3 on page 11 provides a brief overview of these three models.)

Carol Kuhlthau's six-stage model of the information-seeking process conceptualizes how meaning is learned through active participation with information resources. This model encourages an in-depth focus that enables students to seek more relevant information and produce a higher-quality product. Kuhlthau states, "Living in the information age requires people to go beyond the ability to locate information and requires competence in seeking meaning and understanding. More is not necessarily better without skillful guidance from an insightful person [library media specialist]" (708). (Figure 1.4 on page 11 displays this process as it relates to affective, cognitive, and sensorimotor learning.)

Another current, well-known information problem-solving model is the *Big6* approach (www.Big6.com) by Eisenberg and Berkowitz. This process describes the six thinking steps one goes through any time there is an information problem to be solved. Michael Eisenberg explains it this way: "'Brainstorm and narrow' is the essential process for information seeking strategies.... [Students should] brainstorm all possible information sources to meet the task, and then critically determine the best sources for completing the particular task" (22). (An overview of the *Big6* problem-solving model is displayed in Figure 1.5 on page 12.)

The Research Process, developed by Stripling and Pitts, connects information handling and use with subject matter that is essential for learning to occur. Stripling and Pitts discovered that students have little prior knowledge of the information-seeking process, have fragmented understandings of subject knowledge, and do not understand that their information-seeking knowledge depends on content knowledge and vice versa. As a result, school library media specialists should plan instruction specifically to assist students in attaining these skills. Learning experiences should be viewed holistically, recognizing that one area (e.g., information search process) can support other areas (e.g., content knowledge). As Judy Pitts notes, "There are many different, acceptable paths to the same end. Every...[student seemed] to have a different approach to working on a research assignment and organizing information. Each system worked well, but if everyone had been ordered to use one specific approach, many students would have found themselves incredibly frustrated" (23).

6/Reference Skills for the School Library Media Specialist: Tools and Tips

Figure 8.1 Parenthetical Reference (example). Reprinted with permission. From *Reference Skills for the School Library Media Specialist: Tools and Tips,* by Ann Marlow Riedling. Linworth Publishing, 2000.

References

AASL and AECT. *Information Power: Building Partnerships for Learning.*
Chicago: American Library Association, 1988.

Eisenberg, Michael. "Big6 TIPS: Teaching Information Problem Solving:
Information Seeking Strategies." *Emergency Librarian.* 25 (1997): 22.

Katz, William. *Introduction to Reference Work: Information Sources.* 7th ed.
New York: McGraw-Hill, 1997.

Kuhlthau, Carol. "Inside the Search Process: Information Seeking from the User's
Perspectives." *Journal of the American Society for Information Science.*
42 (1991): 361-371.

Kuhlthau, Carol. "Learning in Digital Libraries: An Information Search Approach."
Library Trends. 45 (1997): 708-725.

Penland, Patrick. *Interviewing for Counselor and Reference Librarians.*
Pittsburgh, PA: University of Pittsburgh, 1970.

Pitts, Judy. "Six Research Lessons from the Other Side." *The Book Report.* 11
(1993): 22-24.

Strayer, Joseph, ed. *The ALA Glossary of Library and Information Science.*
Chicago: American Library Association, 1983.

Stripling, B. K., & Pitts, J. *Brainstorms and Blueprints: Teaching Library Research
as a Thinking Process.* Englewood, CO: Libraries Unlimited, 1988.

Whittaker, Kenneth. "Towards a Theory for Reference and Information Services."
Journal of Librarianship. 9 (1977): 49-63.

Woolls, Blanche. *The School Library Media Manager.* 2nd ed. Englewood, CO:
Libraries Unlimited, 1999.

Figure 8.2 Bibliography Page (References) (example). Reprinted with permission. From *Reference Skills for the School Library Media Specialist: Tools and Tips,* by Ann Marlow Riedling. Linworth Publishing, 2000.

- *The bibliography page* appears at the end of your paper and lists all of the sources you cited in your paper. The bibliography is arranged in alphabetical order by author, last name first. If there is no author, alphabetize by the first word of the title. The bibliography page provides all the information your readers will need if they want to find your original sources. See Figure 8.2 for an example of a bibliography page.

With the evolution of technologies (Internet—e-mail, listservs, etc.), proper methods of citing *electronic* information within the text and in the bibliography have evolved. Many people are adept at citing print resources without great difficulty. However, some find it quite difficult to follow the correct form for an Internet source. If the style manual is not current, it might not have instructions for citing the newer technologies. Usually, however, you can find this information on the Internet. Remember, however, that electronic styles are evolving (and most likely will continue to) over time. For example, view the Web site "Citing Electronic Resources," available at *www.ipl.org/ref/QUE/FARQ/netciteFARQ.html*.

In addition to the information in the printed style manual, further information on each style is posted on numerous Internet sites.

Citation Styles

Citation Styles, Plagiarism, and Style Manuals

www.lib.berkeley.edu/TeachingLib/Guides/Citations.html

This site provides a wealth of information on style manuals and citing sources, both print and electronic.

Freelance Writers

http://freelancewrite.about.com/cs/styleguides/index.htm

This Web site offers information about style guides and citing both print and Web sources, as well as numerous links to additional information.

Writing Tips/Tools

http://psychology.about.com/cs/writingtipstools/index.htm

This site includes a wide variety of useful information, such as the APA Crib Sheet, The Elements of Style, Guide for Citing Electronic Information, and MLA Style.

Chicago Manual of Style

The *Chicago Manual of Style* can be used with all subjects and publications, although it is very often used for academic and professional scholarly and non-scholarly publications. It offers two documentation styles, one using notes and bibliographies, the other using author-date citations and reference lists. The Chicago style also provides guidelines for spelling and punctuation; discusses the treatment of numbers, quotations, illustrations, tables, foreign languages, mathematical symbols, abbreviations; and explains the publishing process. Citations are numbered sequentially throughout the book, and each citation corresponds to a numbered note containing publication information about the source cited. Although the *Chicago Manual of Style* gives some advice for documenting information from computerized data services, computer programs, and electronic documents, the information on documenting Internet sources is not complete.

The *Chicago Manual of Style* recommends italicizing certain elements (such as book and journal titles) in the printed text. According to Chicago style, the first note for a given source should include all the information necessary to identify and locate the source: the author's full name, the full title of the book, the editor's name, the place of publication, publisher, the publication date, and page numbers for quoted information. The first line of each note is indented five spaces. The *Chicago Manual of Style* has two citation styles: scientific (for natural sciences and social sciences) and humanities (for fine arts and literature).

Chicago Manual of Style

Explore the following Web sites for additional information about the *Chicago Manual of Style:*

Citation Style for Research Papers

www.liunet.edu/cwis/cwp/library/workshop/citation.htm

This site by the B. Davis Schwartz Memorial Library, titled, "Citation Style for Research Papers," includes APA, Turabian, MLA, Chicago, and AMA [American Medical Association] styles.

The *Chicago Manual of Style* Bibliographic Format for References

www.libs.uga.edu/ref/chicago.html

This site from the University of Georgia Libraries provides examples of citations.

Chicago Manual of Style *(continued)*

The *Chicago Manual of Style: University of Houston Libraries*

http://info.lib.uh.edu/rsa/chicago.htm

From the University of Houston Libraries, this site also provides useful examples of citation styles—and numerous tips.

Chicago Manual of Style **Form Guide**

www.lib.ohio-state.edu/guides/chicagogd.html

This Web site is a form guide and includes examples for both the newer scientific style of citation and the more traditional humanities style.

Chicago Manual of Style **Documentation**

www.fsu.edu/~library/guides/chicago.html

This site, Florida State University, also provides helpful examples for using the Chicago style.

Exercise: *Chicago Manual of Style*

Let's try citing using the *Chicago Manual of Style*. Locate one single-author book, one multiple-author book, one print periodical article, one newspaper article, one chapter from a book, one Web site, and one e-mail. Create a bibliography page with these resources, using the *Chicago Manual of Style*. Use the following worksheet.

One single-author book: _____

One multiple-author book: _____

One print periodical article: _____

One newspaper article: _____

One book chapter: _____

One Web site: _____

One e-mail: _____

Modern Language Association

The Modern Language Association (MLA) citation style is widely used by writers in literature, language studies, and other fields in the humanities. The overall purpose of the MLA style is to allow you to keep texts as readable and as free of disruptions as possible. The *Modern Language Association Style Handbook* (or *Manual*) provides useful information regarding the purposes of research; suggestions for choosing topics; and guidance for creating outlines, bibliographies, advice on spelling, punctuation, abbreviations.

Over 125 scholarly and literary journals, newsletters, and magazines presently use MLA guidelines. MLA style is common not only in the United States, but in numerous other countries, as well. Schools and instructors have adopted the Modern Language Association style for nearly 50 years.

According to the *MLA Handbook*, each text reference to an outside source must point clearly to a specific entry in the list of works cited. The essential elements of an in-text citation are the author's name (or title of source if there is no author), and a page reference, showing where in a source cited material appears. The MLA style concerns itself with the mechanics of writing as well as proper citations.

MLA Style

For additional information regarding the MLA style, visit the following Web sites:

A Guide for Writing Research Papers Based on MLA Documentation

http://webster.commnet.edu/mla.htm

The Humanities Department and Arthur C. Banks, Jr. Library, Capital Community College, Hartford, Connecticut, created this site, addressing research techniques and other beneficial information regarding citations and styles.

Columbia University Press Citation Guides

www.columbia.edu/cu/cup/cgos/idx_basic.html

The University of South Florida owns this site, which discusses MLA style citations of electronic sources.

MLA Style (continued)

OWL Online Writing Lab

http://owl.english.purdue.edu/handouts/research/r_mla.html

Purdue University Online Writing Lab created this Web site. It provides information and examples concerning the use of MLA style.

Exercise: Modern Language Association Style

Now let's give MLA an attempt. Locate one multiple-author book, one Web site, one listserv, one online journal article, and one print newspaper article. Using the Modern Language Association style, create a bibliography of your resources.

Use the following worksheet for assistance.

One multiple-author book: _____

One Web site: _____

One listserv: _____

One online journal article: _____

One print newspaper article: _____

American Psychological Association

The *American Psychological Association Style* (APA) provides documentation advice for writers in the social sciences. It discusses manuscript content and organization, writing style, and manuscript preparation. *The APA Publication Manual* provides hundreds of guidelines about how to format references, statistics, tables, punctuation, and grammar. It also contains writing tips and instructions on formatting manuscripts. APA style focuses on needs of presenting psychological information. It omits general rules explained in widely available style books and examples of usage that have little relevance to the behavioral and social sciences.

APA Style

For additional information, please explore the following Web sites:

Guides to Citation Styles

www.murdoch.edu.au/dirs/citegdes.html

This site is actually a guide to citation styles, including APA. It links to many useful sites that treat APA (and MLA) styles.

APAStyle.org

www.apastyle.org

This Web site contains helpful information about the APA style, including style tips.

Writers' Workshop

www.english.uiuc.edu/cws/wworkshop/

The Writers' Workshop, from the University of Illinois at Urbana-Champaign, summarizes and illustrates the bibliographical formatting rules for APA (and MLA). See Figure 8.4.

Karla's Guide to Citation Style Guides

http://bailiwick.lib.uiowa.edu/journalism/cite.html

Karla's Guide to Citation Style Guides is a Web site that addresses the use of APA, MLA, and Chicago citation styles, along with others extensively.

Exercise: American Psychological Association

Are you ready to try the American Psychological Association (APA) Style? Ok. Locate one single-author book, one no-author book, one online journal article, one print journal article, and one e-mail. Using APA style, create a bibliography page using your resources.

The following worksheet may assist you with this task:

One single-author book: _____

(continued on next page)

Exercise: American Psychological Association (continued)

One no-author book: _____

One online journal article: _____

One print journal article: _____

One e-mail: _____

THE ANNOTATED BIBLIOGRAPHY

Bibliographies have been the topic of this entire chapter. There may be times, however, when you will be required to create an annotated bibliography. What is an annotated bibliography? It is an organized list of sources or citations with a brief note or description (annotation) about each item. So, what is the purpose of an annotated bibliography? Depending on the assignment, an annotated bibliography can serve a number of purposes.

- It reviews the literature on a specific topic.
- It illustrates the quality of your research.
- It informs the reader of the relevance, accuracy, and quality of the sources cited.
- It provides examples of available resources.
- It explores the topic for further research.

Annotations are descriptive and critical; they expose the author's (your) point of view, clarity and appropriateness of expression, and authority. Typically, an annotation is no more than 150 words and follows the bibliographic citation. Each style (APA, MLA, etc.) has its own specific procedure for writing bibliographic annotations (see your style manual). The following is an example of an annotated bibliography using fictitious citations and annotations.

Smith, J.R. (2001). The erosion of traditional family rituals among adolescents. *Psychology Today, 40,* 44–48.

The author, a researcher with Rutgers University, and uses information from surveys of adolescents to test his hypothesis that traditional family rituals among adolescents are not considered "important." He finds his hypothesis strongly supported by both male and female adolescents. In contrast, an earlier study by Jones (cited above) shows that males and females differ greatly in the importance they place on family rituals, with females believing it is vitally important.

Tell, J.O. (2002). Happy days are here again! *American Sociological Review, 101, 444–450.*

Tell explains that adolescents are "happier and more well adjusted" today than they were 50 years ago. He attributes this to their early independence as well as to the support they receive from peers. I do not agree with Tell's opinion, but I believe it is important to consider all points of view.

APA	MLA	Chicago Manual of Style
Has printed manual	Has printed manual	Has printed manual
Based on the Publications Manual of the American Pyschological Association	Based on the Modern Language Association Style Manual	Based on the Chicago Manual of Style
Used for psychology, education, and other social sciences	Used for literature, arts and humanities	Used with all subjects in the "real world" by books, magazine, newspapers, and other non-scholarly publications
Has updated online electronic citation information	Has updated online electronic citation information	Has updated online electronic citation information
Updates regularly	Updates regularly	Updates regularly

Figure 8.3   Comparison of APA, MLA and Chicago Manual of Style © 2002 by Karla Tonella. Reprinted by permission.

CONCLUSION

The overall purpose of citing sources in a research paper is to provide credit to the creator(s) of the information and to allow the reader(s) of your paper access to the information they need to locate your original sources. There are numerous citation styles and manuals, but three basic citation styles are *Chicago Manual of Style, MLA Handbook for Writers of Research Papers*, and the *Publication Manual of the American Psychological Assocaition*. Figure 8.3 summarizes these styles is used for a different type of writing and research. Printed manuals and Internet sites can assist you in learning how to cite your sources properly both within the text (parenthetical references) and in the bibliography page. Citing sources properly is an essential aspect of research.

REFERENCES AND FURTHER READING

Bauman, M. Garrett. 9 November 2001. "The Devilments of Style." *The Chronicle of Higher Education:* B5.

Burke, John. 1999. *Intronet: A Beginner's Guide to Searching the Internet.* New York: Neal-Schuman.

Crane, Beverly E. 2000. *Teaching with the Internet: Strategies and Modes for K–12 Curricula.* New York: Neal-Schuman.

Harmon, Charles. 2000. *Using the Internet, Online Services, and CD-ROMs for Writing Research and Term Papers* (2nd ed.) New York: Neal-Schuman.

Lane, Nancy, Margaret Chisolm, and Carolyn Mateer. 2000. *Techniques for Student Research: A Comprehensive Guide to Using the Library.* New York: Neal-Schuman.

Lathrop, Ann, and Kathleen Foss. 2000. *Student Cheating and Plagiarism in the Internet Era: A Wake-Up Call.* Greenwood Village, CO: Libraries Unlimited.

Publication Manual of the American Psychological Association (5th ed.). 2001. Washington, DC: American Psychological Association.

Quaratiello, Arlene Rodda. 2000. *The College Student's Research Companion* Second edition New York: Neal-Schuman.

Thompson, Leonora C., and Portia G. Williams. 1995. "But I Changed Three Words!" *Clearing House,* 69: 27–29.

University of Chicago Press. 1993. *The Chicago Manual of Style* (14th ed.). Chicago: University of Chicago Press.

Whitley, Peggy, Catherine Olson, and Susan Goodwin. 2001. *99 Jumpstarts to Research: Topic Guides for Finding Information on Current Issues.* Greenwood Village, CO: Libraries Unlimited.

Zeljak, Cathy, 1999. "Electronic Citation Guides." *Problems of Post-Communism,* 46: 59.

Chapter 9

Now That I've Finished the Research, How Do I Write the Paper?

One of the most critical elements when conducting research is organizing information. Look at it this way. What if you awoke one morning and had no "organizational plan" (even in your head)? For starters, you would not know when to brush your teeth, what clothes to wear, what to eat for breakfast, where to go, or how to get there, and so on. Although this is a bit exaggerated, it does point out that organization is critical for everyone. You have now developed a topic, and you have gathered and evaluated the materials you need for your research project. What do you do next? You need a plan to complete the project.

From your organizational scheme, your first step is to develop a thesis statement (discussed in Chapter 2). Following that, you develop *an outline and a rough draft* and, finally, you add the *finishing touches* to your research project. And then? You *present* your research project. How will you present it? Will you merely turn in your paper to the instructor? Will you give a speech? Will you use visual aids, such as transparencies or PowerPoint? The type of presentation will most likely depend on your specific research project and the assignment. Remember, however, that there are numerous methods of presenting information, and you want to choose the most effective method possible. After all, you have already spent many, many hours on your research project.

ORGANIZATION OF INFORMATION

A research project presents the results of your exploration and gathering of appropriate materials on a selected topic. While it is based on the information you have obtained from a wide range of resources, a research project is exclusively yours. At this point, it is important to continue with your research. First organize the information you have obtained. It is helpful to use an organizational format (or template) that is clear and succinct, something that is easy for you to follow. Although this format may differ from individual to individual, it is a necessary part of the research process. The ability to organize ideas is a principal objective of research and education. Effective organization of ideas helps you determine how much to say and whether your topic is broad enough to interest and inform your audience.

Remember, when you gather materials (from any type of resource), always write down specific bibliographic information about the source in case you want to use it as a reference in your paper. The citation should include

- author or creator's name,
- title of the resource,
- place of publication,
- publisher's name,
- date of copyright (year only for books; date, month for newspapers),
- volume and issue number for journals,
- page numbers,
- URL (if applicable and date accessed).

This will save time, because you will not waste it relocating materials to get this information. In addition, it is important to take notes about each source you locate. Answer questions such as the following:

- Does this material fit the topic?
- Is it a scholarly resource?
- Is the information in this source accurate?
- Are there any notable biases in the material?
- Why do I want to use this resource; where will it fit into my research project?

Carry a notebook around with you and write all information down right away. You can later turn it into a word document or enter it into a database. Always paraphrase or summarize the information, stating it in your own words. There are many different kinds of summaries, and they vary according to the degree with which you interpret the resource. Some are pages long, others just one or two sentences. However, for all types of summaries, you are responsible for generally stating in your own words the ideas of another writer. In order to summarize or paraphrase, it is important to:

- read the original text very carefully and
- highlight or underline what you believe are the main points.

It is also helpful to use the author's last name as a "tag" to introduce information, such as, "Jones contends that…". Keep in mind that if you copy and use the information word-for-word, you need to place quotation marks around it.

Outlining

An outline provides an overview of your paper and allows you to quickly see missing elements, irrelevant items, and the structure of your project. A *working outline* might be only an informal list of topics and subtopics that you are thinking of covering in your paper. A *final outline* should enhance the organization and coherence of your research paper. If portions of your outline seem weak in comparison to others, more research may be required to create a sense of balance. Outlines should be organized according to your purposes. Are you trying to show the chronology of some historical development, the cause-and-effect relationship between one phenomenon and another, the process by which something is accomplished, or the logic of some position? Regardless of type of research paper, attempt to bring related material together under general headings and arrange sections so that they relate logically to each other. A final outline can be written as a *topic outline*, in which you use only short phrases to suggest ideas, or as a *sentence outline*, in which you use full sentences to show the development of ideas more fully. Many word-processing programs have outlining features with automatic formatting that make it simple to outline your research paper. Your outline will differ with the type of research paper you are writing. Overall, however, it is best to bring related resources together under common headings and organize divisions so they relate understandably to each other.

The Rough Draft

The next step is to develop a rough draft of your paper. Remember that a rough draft is just that—your first attempt at creating the research paper. You can't expect to do your finest work with only one try. The following are some tips for writing a rough draft:

- Freewrite. Set a period of time and write anything that comes to mind. This helps you open up the ideas you have in your mind.

- Make a list of everything you want to say about the subject. Do not worry about grammar and spelling; those can come later.
- Use lots of examples. Prove your points.
- Many writers write their introductions after they have written the rest of their rough draft. It might be easier to introduce the material after you know what you are saying.

You will look at your work with a more critical eye if you wait a few hours or a day between finishing the rough draft and revising your paper. Think about the following when you are reviewing your rough draft:

- Does your introduction help the reader to know what he or she will be reading?
- Do your ideas flow logically?
- Does your conclusion summarize the main points and offer new insight on the topic?
- Have you found any grammatical errors, such as sentence structure, spelling, and punctuation that will detract from the quality of your paper?
- Have you included a bibliography using the citation style required, and have you cited your sources correctly within the text of your paper?
- Are you keeping an extra copy of your paper (on a floppy disk, Zip drive, or CD)?

It is also helpful to follow these research tactics:

- Develop your personal search strategy and stick with it.
- Keep all of your notes in one folder and label the folder with your name, the title of your research project, and the date.
- Ask for assistance if you need it.
- Always evaluate your resources (print and electronic).
- Paraphrase/summarize all information (you will understand it better later if it is in your own words).
- Keep narrowing your search if necessary.
- Use a wide variety of resources.
- Use scholarly sources as much as possible.
- Always keep copyright and plagiarism in mind.
- Have someone else look at your resources, outline, and rough draft.
- Remember that research and writing is not linear; it is a *circular process*. While you are writing you may discover again and again that more research is required.

Regardless of how you organize information, you must maintain a systematic approach with which you are comfortable.

Exercise: Organization of Information

Visit the following Web site:

Researching and Organizing Your Paper: The Note Card System

http://depts.gallaudet.edu/Englishworks/writing/notecard.html.

This Web site offers a slightly different approach to organizing information. It is always helpful to learn several methods of organization—and use the one that is easiest and most useful for you. Although the thought of using index cards (you know, the ones you buy in the local drug store?) may seem *ancient*, it is actually a pretty good method of keeping track of things. Computer databases are terrific—but you cannot always carry them around with you to revise and update. Therefore, note cards can be useful. Now, let's see if you can stay focused—using the note card system. Assume that your topic is "Gangs and Adolescents":

1. Make a title for each note card, for example, "Gangs in New York City."

2. Write the main idea of the article/information about gangs in New York City.

3. Write subheadings of this topic, if discovered.

4. Write the source title (the name of the resource where you found the information).

5. Include all pertinent bibliographic information: author or creator, title, publisher, place of publication, copyright date, page numbers (if an online resource, the URL, date located, and other information as mentioned previously).

6. Now, organize the cards by topics. For instance, some may be about gangs in general; others about specific types of gangs; others about New York City and gangs.

7. Before beginning to write your research paper, outline your topics (cards) and use them as guides to your writing.

List three ways this organizational system is helpful for you.

1. _____

2. _____

3. _____

IMPROVING YOUR WRITING

Anyone can learn to write better, but it requires time and work. Even a small effort toward improvement can have positive results. The following are several tips to improve your writing ability:

- Take what you are doing seriously. Good writing is important.
- Read—anything and everything you can, whenever you can. The more familiar and comfortable you are with reading and writing, the easier it will become.
- Try to improve your vocabulary. Make it a point to learn a few new words every week or month. A wide vocabulary gives you a better command of the language and more possibilities of expressing your ideas to others. It may be helpful to visit the following Web site:

A.Word.A.Day

www.wordsmith.org/awad/index.html

- Practice writing—letters to friends, a journal—any way you can think of. Practice makes perfect!
- Learn to revise your writing to become more clear and focused.
- Use a dictionary and thesaurus. If you do not know a word, be sure to look it up.
- Control your language—do not let it control you.
- Read what you write aloud. Your ears can tell you much about how you write.
- Simplify and simplify more. Eliminate anything unnecessary.
- Think clearly. When you are tired or distraught, things become fuzzy and unclear. Choose appropriate times to write.
- Avoid writer's block by understanding that it takes time and patience to be a good writer.

THE FINISHING TOUCHES

You have written your paper—or so you think—but don't stop now. No matter how many times you read a completed paper, you are likely to miss many of your most frequent errors. It is helpful to take a break between writing and proofreading. It is also useful to read your paper aloud—so that you read every little word. In addition, sliding a blank sheet of paper down the page as you read encourages you to make a detailed review of your paper. Even the best writers cannot be totally objective about their own work. Therefore, it is wise to do the following:

- Have someone else (or several others) read your paper and provide you with feedback.
- Proofread your paper—several times.
- Edit and write your final revisions.

It might be helpful to think of this in terms of someone else evaluating your work. The "best" work should:

- contain a beginning, middle, and end;
- include an introduction that is clear, focused, complete, and strong, and requires critical-thinking skills;
- show evidence of organization and revision;
- use a variety of carefully selected resources;
- contain information that is supported in numerous and diverse sources;
- be original and written with accuracy, detail, and understanding;
- be free of grammatical errors of all types (spelling, punctuation, consistency of tense, avoidance of clichés, verb agreement, no fragments or run-on sentences, gender-specific pronouns, etc.);
- include a conclusion that is strong and concise; and
- use proper citations within the text and on the bibliography page (according to the required citation style).

The following Web site regarding concept mapping will provide you with additional knowledge about the organization of information…try it out!

Concept Mapping
www.coun.uvic.ca/learn/program/hndouts/map_ho.html

What *is* concept mapping? Concept mapping is a tool for assisting and enhancing many types of thinking and learning. To create a map, write the main idea in the center of the page—for example, a word, a phrase, or a couple of juxtaposed ideas—then place related ideas on branches that radiate from this central idea.

Exercise: Proofreading and Revising

Ask a friend if you may read a research paper that he or she has previously written. Following the evaluation tips provided in this chapter, determine how you would rate this paper and why. Answer the following questions about the research paper:

- Is the information vague or clear?
- Is the paper organized in a logical manner?
- Has the author used a sufficient number of resources to support the topic?
- Are the materials that are used diverse and scholarly?
- Are there any grammatical errors?
- Does it include an introduction and conclusion that are strong and clear?
- Are the citations written correctly?
- Did you learn anything by reading this paper?
- How do you rate this paper? (1–10, 10 being the best): _____

Discuss your rating: _____

_____

PRESENTING YOUR RESEARCH

Your research paper is a compilation of the essential facts and ideas on a topic that have been gathered from a variety of resources. The information collected about your research topic should be presented in *your* perspective. This will make your research project an original, creative presentation of a familiar body of information. There are numerous ways to present a paper, using various resources and equipment. How you will present the paper may depend on a number of factors such as:

- amount of time permitted,
- resources and materials available,
- size of the audience,
- size and arrangement of the room,
- constraints imposed by the delivery medium or audience,
- type of information being communicated,
- expertise and background of the audience, and
- manner in which the audience is expected to use the information.

In addition, your particular topic may lend itself better to one method than another. Physical information (such as location) is often best communicated graphically; graphics are also better suited to conveying information about individual objects. For example, if your research topic is bats, it might be useful to use visuals to show how bats sleep and the features of their wings.

Outlines are useful tools in planning *and delivering* a presentation. A *planning outline* helps in determining the organizational sequence that makes the most sense for presenting a particular topic to a given audience. It is more detailed in that it not only labels the parts, but it also describes subpoints and shows relationships between major ideas. A *presentation outline* assists you during the presentation. It is much briefer than a planning outline because its purpose is only to provide cues that help you "stay on track" during the presentation. Regardless of the presentation type, all presentations should accomplish the following:

- They should present the research information in a logical, interesting sequence that the audience can follow.
- They should provide information that is accurate, clear, and appropriate.

If visuals are included, be certain that the graphics reinforce the research, that the visual information is accurate, and that the graphics are large and clear enough for everyone to see. If you use video or audio, be certain that they enrich the presentation and convey meaning without being too lengthy. Also, remain cognizant of smooth transitions. Transitions are like bridges between parts of your presentation. Pause during a transition, and choose your words carefully. For example, if you are showing comparison, use words such as "in contrast" or "compared to." It is sometimes useful to repeat yourself, such as "as I have noted previously." Examples are also useful; if you use an example, preface it with "for instance" or "to illustrate." Finally, to summarize or conclude a presentation, use phrases such as, "on the whole" or "in conclusion." If you are presenting orally, use a clear voice and correct and precise pronunciation of all terms. In addition, maintain as much eye contact with the audience as possible.

Exercise: Reflection

It is always wise to reflect on your work and to evaluate what you have done. You should review your progress throughout the research process to identify what caused you difficulty and to determine things you might do differently to improve the process as well as the presentation of your findings. Think about the following questions as they relate to your research experience:

- What was your most helpful resource? What was your least helpful resource? What made them useful or not useful?
- What parts of this activity were most challenging?
- What was the most important thing you learned about conducting research?
- How will you do it differently next time?
- What is one new research skill that you acquired or efficient method you discovered because of this project?

CONCLUSION

Effective organization of information is critical to a high-quality research paper. Develop an organizational plan with which you are comfortable. Remember to create an outline first, followed by a rough draft. Before finalizing your paper, proofread it, have others read it, then edit and revise. Beginning to write a research paper is the most difficult part, and organization is the key to success. Presentation of your final paper should be "the icing on the cake." This is your opportunity to show others what you have accomplished.

Your research project is finished! You have now learned the process—from beginning to end—of creating and presenting a research paper. You are information literate and have *learned to learn*.

Webliography

Grammar and Punctuation

Grammar Handbook

   www.english.uiuc.edu/cws/wworkshop/grammarmenu.htm

Common Writing Mistakes

   www.hamilton.edu/academic/Resource/WC/ComMistakes.html

The Topic

Analyzing Your Topic

   www-english.tamu.edu/wcenter/invention.html

Planning and Starting the Writing Assignment

A Model for Academic Writing

   www2.colgate.edu/diw/model.html

When You Start to Write

   http://owl.english.purdue.edu/handouts/general/gl_plan2.html

Title, Introduction, and Conclusion

Developing an Introduction

   http://leo.stcloudstate.edu/acadwrite/intro.html

Strategies for Writing a Conclusion

   http://leo.stcloudstate.edu/acadwrite/conclude.html

Writing Style and Technique

Constructing Paragraphs

http://owl.english.purdue.edu/handouts/general/gl_essay.html

Strategies for Reducing Wordiness

http://leo.stcloudstate.edu/style/wordiness.html

Gender-free Writing

http://leo.stcloudstate.edu/style/genderbias.html

Revising and Rewriting

Editing and Proofreading Strategies

http://leo.stcloudstate.edu/acadwrite/genproofed.html

Citing Sources

Using Sources for a Research Paper

www.hamilton.edu/academic/Resource/WC/UsingOutsideSources.html

Using APA Format

http://owl.english.purdue.edu/handouts/research/r_apa.html

Using MLA Format

http://owl.english.purdue.edu/handouts/research/r_mla.html

Glossary

Abstract: A brief summary of a book, article, or Web site.

Annotation: A paragraph for each information source cited in a bibliography that summarizes the important findings and conclusions in that source.

APA: (American Psychological Association): A citation style that is used most often by writers and students in the sciences and social sciences.

Bias: Prejudice; an inclination or preference that inhibits impartiality.

Bibliography: A list of the resources you use when researching your paper.

Boolean Logic: A way to combine terms using "operators" such as AND, OR, and NOT. AND requires that all terms appear in a record. OR retrieves records with either term. NOT excludes terms.

Browser: A software program that makes it possible to view World Wide Web documents. It translates HTML-encoded files into the text, images, sounds, and other feature you see. Examples are Netscape and Internet Explorer.

Call Number: Letters and numbers assigned to a book according to its subject to indicate its location on the shelf.

CD-ROM: The acronym for Compact Disc-Read Only Memory. Computer storage discs that can contain vast amounts of information.

Chicago Manual of Style: A citation style that can be used primarily for scholarly publications.

Citations: Brief publication information about a book, article, Web site, and or other resource. Citations usually include the author, title, publisher, and copyright date.

Citing: The process of giving credit to the information sources used to write a paper or develop a presentation.

Copyright: Legal ownership of a work that provides the creator of a work the sole right to publish and sell that work.

Cross Reference: A direction from one term or heading to another. A SEE reference indicates that all materials will be found listed under another specific term; a SEE ALSO reference lists other terms under which related materials might be found.

Deep (or Invisible) Web: Content that is stored in databases accessible on the Web, but not available via search engines.

Dewey Decimal Classification System (DDC): A classification system used primarily in school and small public libraries that is based on ten main classes.

Directory: A directory is a system that a computer uses to organize files on the basis of specific information. Directories can be organized hierarchically so that files can appear in a number of different ways, such as the order in which they were created, alphabetically by name or by type, and other ways.

Domain: A scheme for indicating logical and sometimes geographical venues of a Web page from the network. Examples are .edu (education), .com (commercial), .gov (government).

Edition: All copies of a book printed from one typesetting without substantial change. A revised edition is a corrected and updated edition based on the original with modifications.

Editor: The person responsible for compiling and organizing a periodical or a book written by several authors.

Fair Use: Fair use grants particular types of users conditional rights to use or reproduce certain copyrighted materials if the reproduction or use meets specific guidelines.

Final Outline: Similar to a working outline, but containing more complete information on the research topic.

Full-Text: The complete text of a book, article, or Web site.

Handbook: A reference work that serves as a handy guide to a particular subject.

HTML: Hypertext Markup Language. This is a standardized language of computer code, imbedded in "source" documents behind all Web documents, containing the textual content, images, links to other documents, and formatting instructions for display on the screen.

Hypertext: On the World Wide Web this feature allows a text area, image, or other object to become a "link" (like a chain) that retrieves other computer files on the Internet.

Interlibrary Loan: A cooperative agreement among libraries willing to share their books and other resources with each other.

Internet: A network that connects computers worldwide.

Internet Paper Mill: A Web site that allows you to directly purchase or download research papers online.

Introduction: The first part of a research paper that introduces the audience to the subject about which the paper is being written.

Journal: A scholarly or professional periodical.

Keyword: A word searched for in a search command. Keywords are searched in any order.

Librarian's Index: A subject directory that is compiled by library experts.

Library Catalogs (also called OPACs): An organized and searchable record of all the materials that a particular library owns.

Library of Congress Classification System (LC): A classification system used in large (primarily public and academic libraries) to arrange their materials.

Library Policies and Procedures: Critical documents to help assure that libraries can operate efficiently and effectively and to protect and assist all library users.

Link: The URL imbedded in another document, so that if you click on the highlighted text or button referring to the link, you retrieve the outside URL.

Match-All Search: This type of search is similar to Boolean searching, but in place of AND a plus sign (+) is used; in place of NOT a minus sign (−) is used.

Meta-Search Engine: These are search engines that automatically submit your keyword search to several other search tools and retrieve results from all their databases.

MLA (Modern Language Association): A citation style that is most often used by writers and students in the humanities, languages, and literature disciplines.

OPAC (Online Public Access Catalog): This is a general term for a library's electronic catalog.

Paraphrase: Re-wording or summarizing someone else's words or ideas.

Parenthetical References: Writing sources cited on your bibliography page within the paper itself.

Peer Review: Process in which experts in the field read, review, and evaluate articles based on certain criteria before recommending them for publication.

Periodical: Any information source that is issued regularly, for example, daily, weekly, monthly, or quarterly. This includes newspapers, magazines, and journals.

Periodical Database: A searchable index to periodicals, such as newspapers, magazines, and journals.

Personal (Home) Page: A Web page created by an individual, as opposed to a page created for an institution, business, organization, or other entity.

Phrase Searching: A type of search that uses more than one keyword enclosed in quotations (" "). It is sometimes called a character string.

Plagiarism: The act of copying or paraphrasing someone else's text or ideas without giving them credit.

Preface: A section of a book that includes the purpose, scope, and organization. The preface tells why the book was written and what is to come next in the text.

Protocol: This is the standard or set of rules that two computers use to communicate with each other. Also known as a communications protocol or network protocol, a set of such standards ensures that different network products or programs can work together. Any product that uses a given protocol should work with any other product using the same protocol.

Public Domain: A storehouse of all works that are not protected by copyright.

Reference Material: A book or other work designed to be consulted rather than read completely; generally a source that must be used within a library.

Robot (or Spider): A program designed to automatically go out and explore the Internet for a specific purpose. Robots that record and index all of the contents of the network to create searchable databases are sometimes called *spiders*. WebCrawler and Lycos are examples of robots.

Rough Draft: A first attempt at writing a research paper.

Scope: The breadth and depth of what is covered and in what detail in a resource.

Search Engine: An automated, controlled system that enables users to search for Web pages on a selected topic by entering keywords.

Search Statement: A set of instructions or a group of keywords used to locate appropriate information.

Sentence Outline: An outline that uses full sentences to show the development of ideas more fully.

Serial: Any publication issued on an ongoing basis, usually published at regular intervals and intended to be continued indefinitely. A periodical is one type of serial.

Subject Directory: A human-controlled system that enables users to browse through subject categories for information.

Subject Heading: A word or group of words under which all materials on a particular topic are listed in a card catalog, OPAC, or in an index.

Summarize: Similar to paraphrase, but provides information even closer to your own words than the words of the author or creator.

Synonyms: Two or more words or expressions that have the same, or nearly the same, meaning in some or all senses.

Thesaurus: A book of words and their synonyms.

Thesis Statement: The narrow conclusion you make based on the information gathered for a research paper. It is an assertion; not a statement of fact.

Title Page: Typically the first page in a book that tells the author, title, illustrator, and publisher.

Title Searching: A search method that allows one to search with the HTML title of a Web page.

Topic Outline: An outline that uses only short phrases to suggest ideas.

Truncation: A search technique using a symbol (usually an asterisk) at the end of a word in order to retrieve all of its possible endings.

URL (Universal Resource Locator): This is the most basic information about where a Web page is located on the World Wide Web. It includes information about what Web server the page is stored, in which directory it is located, its name, and the protocol used to retrieve it.

Verso Page: The page on the reverse side of the title page that includes information such as the copyright date, author, title, publisher, and other aspects of publication.

Virtual Library: A managed collection of information resources and services available electronically via the Internet.

Volume: An individual book; whatever is found in one binding. For a periodical, a volume is the collective unit for a set of issues. Frequently a volume is one year's worth of issues.

Wildcards: A search technique that typically uses the question mark symbol in place of a letter in a word.

Working Outline: An informal list of topics and subtopics associated with a research paper.

WWW (The World Wide Web): A portion of the Internet that presents textual and multimedia information in page format.

Yahoo!: Currently the largest and most well-known subject directory.

Index

About the Author

Ann Marlow Riedling is a graduate of Indiana University with a bachelor's degree in education, graduate of the University of Georgia with a master's degree in library science and educational technology; and a graduate of the University of Louisville with a doctorate in educational administration and information technology. She has worked in library science and educational technology since 1974, and she is currently serving as associate professor and departmental chair of School Library and Information Science at Spalding University, Louisville, Kentucky. Ann has published two previous textbooks: *Reference Skills for the School Library Media Specialist* and *Catalog It!* She served the academic year 1999/2000 as a Fulbright Scholar in Bahrain, Yemen, and Egypt, teaching and consulting in information science. Her areas of research and interest include distance education, information literacy, young adult literature, and school reference services.